Disordered
---- LOVES ----

---- Healing ----
the
Seven Deadly Sins

William S. Stafford

COWLEY PUBLICATIONS
Cambridge ✦ Boston
Massachusetts

Published in the United States of America by Cowley Publications, a division of the Society of St. John the Evangelist. No portion of this book may be reproduced, stored in or introduced into a retrieval system, or transmitted, in any form or by any means—including photocopying—without the prior written permission of Cowley Publications, except in the case of brief quotations embodied in critical articles and reviews.

Library of Congress Cataloging-in-Publication Data:
    Stafford, William S.
       Disordered loves: healing the seven deadly sins/
        William S. Stafford
       p.   cm.
       ISBN 1-56101-090-1 (alk. paper)
       1. Deadly sins. 2. Sin. 3. Spiritual life—Christianity. I. Title.
      BV4626.S77 1994   241'.3—dc20   93-43282

Scripture quotations are taken from the Revised Standard and the New Revised Standard versions of the Bible, and from the 1979 Book of Common Prayer.

Cover illustration is a detail from the panels of Adam and Eve by Lucas Cranach the Elder, ca. 1472, located in the Uffizi Gallery in Florence.

This book is printed on recycled, acid-free paper and was produced in the United States of America.

Cowley Publications
28 Temple Place
Boston, Massachusetts 02111

To my wife, Barbara,
And to my parents,
Chase and Harriette Grace Stafford,
who have taught me a great deal about sin
and God's mercy.

---- Contents ----

---- Acknowledgements ----

The clergy and people of several parish churches listened
and responded thoughtfully to my lenten addresses about the
seven deadly sins: Grace Church in Alexandria, St. Mary's
Church in Arlington, Good Shepherd Church in Burke, Holy
Comforter Church in Vienna, Virginia, and the American Ca-
thedral in Paris. I thank them all for letting me think out
loud with them and for their lively reactions, out of which
this book grew.

My brother, Tim Stafford, my wife, Barbara, and my colleague, Mary Sulerud, read various drafts. Robert Prichard,
Katherine Berry, Jennifer Stafford, and David Brown read
versions of one particularly recalcitrant chapter. My editor,
Cynthia Shattuck, brought a surgeon's acuity and a poet's ear
to her work on the manuscript as a whole. Thanks to them all
for their help and encouragement.

Chapter 1

What Is Sin?

One Saturday during my junior year in college, I went on a field trip to Half Moon Bay, on the California coast. For a long time I had loved the Pacific shore—fog and bright blue sky flowing back and forth daily, changeless green sea heaving against brown rocks, wildflowers and loneliness—but that day my geology professor gave me a new way to see it all. The bus set us down near a stream issuing through a cliff to the beach. We got geological maps along with instructions to draw and write a history of the stream valley. I worked hard, peering at rocks and exploring the shape of the land around them. Soon I had to scramble to the maps and the textbooks in order to find words for what I was seeing. Suddenly the coastline became something with its own history, with a past and a future. I could tell what some of that past was: eons during which sediment had settled into rock, then the great plain was lifted up above the sea, eaten away into seacliffs, eroded by the stream that shaped the soft hills above and the sharp gully leading to the beach. None of the old beauty vanished, but a disturbing, exciting new beauty broke open from the landscape before me. I had new words and new eyes for a familiar reality.

Twenty years after that field trip, a massive earthquake ripped through the area. Great plates shifted as roads split and hillsides came down. At the Marina District in San Francisco, a few miles to the north, people had for generations built wonderfully bizarre houses in pastel colors standing clear and fresh on straight flat streets by the bay. They had paid no mind to geological maps, had no eyes to see or words to speak about the history of the earth under their feet, but that ignorance had a price. The Marina District is built on old hardened mud and rubble, many feet deep. When seismic shock hits mud and rubble, it turns to mush. Houses collapsed, people died, terrible fires burned. Having no eyes and no words for reality has a price.

— Recovering a Lost Language —

At times a whole culture may forget how to see and speak of significant human realities. Yet those forgotten things will not go away, even though the concepts, the vocabulary, and the perspective may vanish. Nothing replaces them; a significant part of human life is simply lost to view. The culture loses beauties it no longer has the means to imagine, and is left oblivious to real threats.

"Sin" is a word that is vanishing from our culture's vocabulary now. The editors of dictionaries have not yet ruled it archaic and restricted it to the limbo of unabridged editions. Yet the word "sin" is a step into an older language that Americans passively retain but do not actively use outside church. To those who do not go to church, "sin" is a code word for the whole mass of superstition that the modern world has thrown off. Almost no one uses "sin" in the sense of a knife that could probe a wound or a lens that could bring some distortion into sharp focus. Educated people speak of weaknesses, crises, mistakes, even personality disorders, but not of sins. Using "sin" to describe corporate life, the life of a nation or family or neighborhood, is even more infrequent. It is not employed in politics or public affairs at all, although the ghost of "sin" still haunts purely religious talk.

Yet only a century ago, "sin" was one term within a rich and complex language for realities of the human world now left unexpressed. Marks of that language are still to be seen here and there. Go to the Lincoln Memorial in Washington, D.C. and look to the right of the deep eyes of the giant statue. There stands a white marble wall where one of Lincoln's speeches is incised, a speech given when America was in the stench of blood and smoke from the worst war ever fought on our soil, fought over the claim of some Americans to own other Americans as their property.

> If we shall suppose that American Slavery is one of those offenses which, in the providence of God, must needs come, but which, having continued through His appointed time, He now wills to remove, and that He gives to both North and South, this terrible war, as the woe due to those by whom the offense came, shall we discern therein any departure from those divine attributes which the believers in a Living God always ascribe to Him? Fondly do we hope—fervently do we pray—that this mighty scourge of war may speedily pass away. Yet, if God wills that it continue, until all the wealth piled by the bond-man's two hundred and fifty years of unrequited toil shall be sunk, and until every drop of blood drawn with the lash, shall be paid by another drawn with the sword, as was said three thousand years ago, so still it must be said: "the judgments of the Lord, are true and righteous altogether."

When Lincoln spoke those words, Americans could still understand them. The mysterious reality of God's judgment on human sin through a "mighty scourge of war" could still be named in the public forum and those names be understood. The heart of his speech was this: both South and North had long denied the reality that slavery was sin. Yet God would not tolerate sin forever, whether people recognized his will or not. The disaster gripping America was the direct result of that long-ignored reality.

Several implications of that message were obvious to Lincoln's hearers but not to us. First, his language about the nation's sin was interleaved with language about God. Sin only shows up in proximity to God. Indeed, the word took its meaning from its relation to God. Slavery was not sinful simply because whites were committing an open injustice against blacks; it was sinful because they did it in God's face. Humans were accountable to God for what they did, and it was sin against God when they failed in that account. Conscience, moral right, judgment, guilt: all were related to God. Without God, there is no sin. Our culture, over a century later, has lost that sense of accountability to God and so the language of sin is disappearing.

Second, Lincoln's audience knew that God was actively if mysteriously at work among human lives. History was the loom on which God wove truth, as hard as it might be to see the pattern. Real sin brought real judgment in the end—actions have consequences in God's world. For one thing, sin ruined good things. Lincoln's speech did not dwell on how much positive human goodness and beauty had been stifled by enslaving Africans; in this he may have been blinded in part by the racist assumptions he shared with most of the American populace. But Lincoln was utterly clear about the overt wrong of slavery, and the weight of that wrong in history. Its injustice deserved the bloodshed at Manassas and Gettysburg. In God's time, sin would come to a reckoning. In our age, however, we hardly think of history as shaped by God's will.

Third, the language of sin was corporate as well as individual. Lincoln assumed that the sin of slavery implicated the whole nation. It never occurred to him that individual slaveholders could escape personal guilt by putting the blame on impersonal economic forces or on their culture, nor that people who had not themselves owned slaves could proclaim their innocence and stand back from the nation's disgrace. Slavery was a sin that a whole people had committed, and for which God was holding a whole people accountable. In our own culture, sin has shrunk to mean a purely individual moral fault.

Last of all, the vocabulary of sin was public. Lincoln used it as President, addressing the whole nation at his official inauguration. It did not occur to him that the separation of church and state meant that an elected official could not own the nation's guilt before God. Politics had to deal with reality, and both God and sin were real. For us now, however, the idea of sin is rigorously excluded from public affairs.

Lincoln's assumptions about this common vocabulary of sin were widely shared in his world. In reading diaries or letters from the last century, it is clear that sin and the rich vocabulary associated with it offered language that men and women could use to bring their lives into focus. One might desert one's family for a new sexual partner; nineteenth-century novelists could evoke the ambiguities of such a decision. Yet the vocabulary of sin still always applied to it. It was not sufficient to call it a mid-life crisis or an act of self-liberation.

There are some exceptions to the shrinking and marginalization of the language of sin. Martin Luther King, Jr., used explicitly Jewish and Christian terms to force Americans to recognize that racism was a sin against God and against neighbor. As King preached to America, he pushed overtly religious language into an area of life from which much of white America had resolutely excluded it for centuries, a racist wall now moated by secularization. But that partial victory of an older language was not free from ambiguity. Some who followed in King's train, and who have since pushed for other forms of social liberation, were uncomfortable with talk about the "sin" of denying that black people are made "in God's image." They were content to push for absolute individual self-determination among all people. One did not need a God to be self-determining; there was no meaning to "sin" in the autonomist's vocabulary. The tide of secularization has washed back.

That tide, however, has an authentic moral force that Christians must not ignore. One of the major powers behind secularization has been its passionate demand that religion be exiled because of the harm it does and because it is not true. Lincoln made his America swallow a bitter fact: many Christians were teaching as a biblical principle that God approved of slavery. Religious language could help to enslave people. A century earlier, the French *philosophe* Voltaire claimed that he ran a fever annually, when he remembered Catholics butchering Protestants on St. Bartholomew's Eve in service of their "truth." It was all an illusion anyway, in Voltaire's view; Catholics had as much reason to worship their communion bread as Tibetans had to adore the dung of the Dalai Lama. Human beings are such fragile crockery; why break them over nonsense?

Christians may wish to discount the anti-religious cynicism of Voltaire's heirs. Yet what of the many cases in which Christians did injure their neighbors? Or what of the times when they defined "sin" to include actions that were not wrong at all? Recently a white teenager confessed to a colleague of mine the "sin" of kissing a black man. Having sexual desire or experiencing anger has often been called sinful. Slaves were taught that any disobedience to their masters was sin. Has not "sin" (together with the whole Christian vocabulary) been used by the powerful to protect their interests?

It is obviously true that each culture and generation has distinctive spiritual insights, and equally distinctive blind spots. The seeds of moral life grow, and are shaped in their growing, by the soil of their own day. In one particular generation they may flourish in some ways and be stunted in others. In another generation or place they may grow quite differently. They are never entirely wholesome. I hold Robert E. Lee in honor. The dining room of my house is one he visited often in his day, and I hope that a little of his grace and loyalty of character is shared there now. But the priority Lee placed on loyalty to Virginia led him to spend his honor in a cause which, at the end, amounted to the claim of whites to enslave blacks. He would have thought it sinful for him not to defend Virginia's laws by force of arms.

The fact that there are perversions of moral insight, however, does not discredit all moral insight. If some people have views of sin which are themselves sinful, that does not mean that sin does not exist or that the whole tradition needs to be discarded. The very ability of critics to detect others' self-service and false moralism depends on true moral insight.

Ironically, it is the spiritual tradition flowing from the prophets of Israel that has made Westerners so adept at criticizing their own religious tradition with a passion later inherited by the Enlightenment. That human beings invent ideas and values and myths to uphold their own unjust interests was detected long before Voltaire. John Calvin called it "idolatry." People, he believed, have an inexhaustible capacity for inventing gods to please themselves, with moral standards that conveniently mirror the natures of those false gods. Calvin thought, for example, that the medieval clergy had deliberately perverted Christianity to assure themselves of steady income and secure power. By the priests' (idolatrous) standards, "piety" for layfolk meant keeping priests fat and happy. And others could play at the same game. Rich people had their own god to serve: their money. Not surprisingly, their highest moral value was the defense of property. This idolatry, Calvin thought, was difficult to detect, since human society as a whole simply assumed that the idols were in fact divine. If exposed, they still were difficult to dethrone; people had a powerful interest in maintaining them.

Christian tradition clearly recognizes that some talk about sin can itself be sinful. Calvin was not alone in thinking so; he drew on a long tradition. He had learned it from Luther and Bernard of Clairvaux and Augustine, and Augustine from Paul, and Paul from Jeremiah and Ezekiel. If some of the religious language of Christians is twisted, however, the answer need not be to throw all of it out. In a tradition as long and diverse as Christianity, one part may correct the perversions and blindnesses of another. We might teach Thomas Aquinas something about the full humanity of women; he might teach us something about loving truth.

By the time Lincoln wrote his second inaugural address, enlightened criticism had already pushed some kinds of Christian language off the public stage. In spite of his deep reflection on the matter of sin, he did not actually use the word "sin." And although he spoke of blood, it was the blood drawn by the lash or by the sword, not the blood shed on Jesus' cross. Yet his audience still knew where sin and blood and God came together, at the center. In particular, enslaved African Christians knew that center:

> Were you there when they crucified my Lord?
> Were you there when they crucified my Lord?
> O! Sometimes it causes me to tremble,
>   tremble, tremble!
> Were you there when they crucified my Lord?

They knew plenty about idolatry: not so much their African ancestors' worship of lesser gods, but their American masters' construction of a false morality in which a false god blessed slavery. It was not hard for people vulnerable to the whip and the rope to understand that the true God might come among his people as one to be beaten and hanged by those who meant to hold on to their idols.

— Sin and the Cross —

In principle, Christians have always known that Jesus' death on the cross was the very heart and center of sin. The deep rebellion against God joined in by all humans at all times, which is the core of idolatry, asserted itself decisively when Jesus was killed. He had asserted God's sole kingdom. Those who denied it and rebelled against it, who meant to keep control of their own world, executed him. To God, they spoke the whole human race's ultimate "no." When God raised Jesus from the dead, God forgave the final sin; he turned humanity's "no" into his own final "yes." A completely new possibility for human life dawned on Easter.

Some years ago I was driving up the valley of a little Yorkshire river, the Rye. Past some muddy hedges, against the gray sky, I saw ruins rise, carved stones standing in lines through acres of thick grass. They were the remains of an old monastery named Rievaulx. I had read books written by the monks who had once lived there, but their ruined home was strange to me. I got out, disoriented; broken corridors and walls stretched out around me, and I could not tell one from another. The guidebook's little map was no help, since I could not connect its diagram with the lines of stones around me. Turning around, however, I saw great arches standing above everything else, and picked my way through to them. It was the abbey church. Open to the sky, its walls still formed the outline of a great cross in the green grass. I walked to the center of that cross, facing the rise where once the high altar had stood. I could see the cross shape on my map, and I knew where I was. The lines of stone around me and the lines printed on the map converged. X marked the spot.

The old monks of Rievaulx had gathered at that X for the Eucharist, to reenact the central event of Jesus' death. "This is my body, which is given for you. This is my blood, which is shed for you and for many *for the forgiveness of sins.*" When

Christians gather for their chief act of worship, where their whole grammar of reality comes together in one direct language spoken with God, the center is obvious. The center is an event, and whatever else Christians say about sin is formed by it. The whole labyrinth of sin, sins of all descriptions and all kinds, stretches out from that central X.

As Lincoln's hearers knew, as those monks knew, sin is the refusal of human beings to let God be God; it is the decision to create a false center for life, an idol, to which we give our ultimate loyalty. Sin coalesced in purest form when Jesus was rejected and executed. That is what a "sinner" is: someone who is part of our race's ingenious efforts to live without the true God, someone who will not stand at the X and accept God's offer of a new possibility through Jesus. If that defines "sin" and "sinner" in the Christian vocabulary, however, then what are discrete "sins"?

Through baptism into Jesus' death and resurrection, Christians have been led out from their old idolatrous lives into a new way of being. They have renounced solidarity with the old conspiracy; the new unity with Jesus has begun. That means, as Paul says, that we have died to sin, so that we may live to Christ. Yet, somehow, not all of the old ties are broken. Some loyalties remain.

When I was a boy, I was not much of an athlete or a fighter, although I would have given a lot to be either. My school playground, in a tough neighborhood outside of New York City, was the scene of a good many ballgames and a good many battles. My classmates considered me too shortsighted to play ball or to fight well, though they did beat me up when they had nothing better to do. But when I went home and walked through the door that led into the kitchen, everything changed. It was warm. My mother was glad to see me. I mattered, and I didn't need to fight for approval or win games for love. It was a different world, a total contrast. "Outdoors" was a different order of life from "indoors."

Yet the contrast was not quite total. Inside the door of my home, I found that I could round up my little brother and sisters and get them to play the games or fight the fights I lost at school. I was sure to win against them! I had not left my envy and anger outside at the playground. I brought the outdoors indoors.

It does not take much insight to see that what the New Testament calls "the present age" is still very present, even for those who are baptized. One has to live in a world shaped by the old arrangements every day, and in turn they inevitably shape one's mind and heart. But in another way, the old arrangements were already inside. Not everything gets left behind in the baptismal water.

In some respects we are still in solidarity with the old order of things. The "old Adam," as Paul calls it, still acts as if it were alive; the "old yeast" threatens to sour the dough. The sneaking thought of ourselves as gods, solitary and autonomous, still lives within us and our communities. Christians have debated fiercely as to whether that constant tug toward solidarity with the old order of sin should itself be called sin. What few have doubted is that the actions that spring from it and the dispositions of character that are rooted in it themselves deserve the name of "sins."

An *action* can be sinful because it expresses solidarity with the old rebellion. Not long ago at my son's soccer game, on a hot, sticky day, I went to the far side of the field because there was some shade. Over there, on the other team's side, I continued to whoop and holler for my team. The opposing coach quite rightly found this obnoxious, and told me either to shut up or to change sides. I didn't like that very much. But the point was clear: I was standing on one side, but acting as if I were on the other. Christians do it all the time—when they do, it is called sin, whether it is a Christian individual or a Christian community. Because the decision or action expresses solidarity with the old order of sin against God, it is called a sin.

Actions and decisions do not simply express a preexisting direction of our lives and identities, however; they help create that direction. They shape one's character. If you commit a murder, you will never be the same person again. If you cheat on a civil service examination, the rest of your career will be built on that lie. The whole approach of the tobacco industry to the results of cancer research has been determined by their prior decision to go ahead and market cigarettes regardless. An action or decision may not simply express solidarity with sin; it may actually create and maintain that solidarity. What we do, as individuals and as communities, helps to make us what we will be. If I act in a way that identifies me decisively with the old order, I shape my character in ways that deny God's new possibility.

There is another consideration. Actions are themselves a kind of language, expressing to others what the actor thinks and wants. If I decide not to vote in the presidential election, that communicates my evaluation of American politics. In more subtle ways, our actions teach others about God. What happens to the children of abusive or indifferent parents? The love of mother and father is meant to draw a child into full human personality; the failure of that love may wound beyond healing. But it does not only hurt the psyche. Abused children in later life often have a terribly difficult time understanding God's love. Their parents' behavior ought to have taught them, in a reflecting, symbolic way, what God is like. The children have learned, all right: they have learned that the core of the universe will reject them, hurt them, treat them like trash. Human love is meant to be a sign of God's; loving actions are a kind of alphabet that spells God's name. Sinful actions spell the name of a false god.

Actions, therefore, may be sins, but they do not usually come out of thin air. Human beings and human communities have a *character* that disposes them to act in a certain way. If you are disposed to be impatient, you are more likely to lean on your horn in heavy traffic. A man who has been brought up to have contempt for women may be able to keep his mouth shut and hold back from contemptuous actions, but few such men find it easy. Dispositions, in other words, may shape people toward sinful actions. When Jesus looked at people's deeds, he was most interested in what they revealed about the heart within. He saw concrete sins as the natural expression of a corrupt heart, a heart disposed to reject God.

The monks of Rievaulx knew that well. They had come to the monastery because their baptism's work was not complete. Through all of the books they wrote, there is a yearning for God, an ache for the holiness and purity of God they did not yet fully share. When they came to the cross daily, they were very aware of the dispositions that continued to shape their characters apart from God. The whole life of Rievaulx was designed to bring them to the cross continuously, to place them in the full current of God's love, so that the old dispositions might be dissolved and the life of Christ grow up in them. To help them understand that long work of repentance, they drew on an old tradition classifying sinful dispositions into seven groups: the "seven deadly sins." Gluttony, lust, avarice, anger, envy, accidie, pride: those are seven names for the sinful forces within us, the dispositions that move us away from solidarity with God and deform the image of God within us.

This list of seven deadly sins was hammered out over centuries of accumulated Christian experience. As such, the list of seven is not found in the Bible itself. Yet it grew out of the response to Scripture by men and women who were seeking grace to reshape their characters and communities toward God and neighbor. The first versions come from the fifth century, out of the deserts of Egypt. There, hermits and monastic communities were struggling to root out the sinful patterns that distracted them and kept them from giving themselves wholly to the contemplation of God. Later, throughout the middle ages, these categories of sinful dispositions were developed in fresh ways so that they could be used by all groups and social classes in the work of self-examination and repentance that prepared the whole Christian people for Easter each year. Some Christian communities use them still. A millennium and a half of Christian experience of sin has been crystallized in the seven deadly sins.

A modern translation might be seven terminal spiritual illnesses, for the seven deadly sins refer to breakdowns or weaknesses, sicknesses or forces within people and communities that tend to deliver them over to the old order of sin and death. Each one may give rise to specific actions of a thousand different kinds, to certain attitudes and habits of being, or to all sorts of blindness and deafness of spirit. Different people and communities suffer more severely from some of the deadly sins than from others; few are immune from all of them.

First in the list comes *gluttony*: sin in relation to eating one's daily bread. Then comes *lust*, the expression of sin through human sexual life. *Avarice*, or covetousness, is next: the deformation of our desire to possess material things, and by implication, sin's twisting of the whole economic order. These first three of the seven are closely related to the material, bodily side of human life.

The next two sins cut deeper, to the capacity of humans to relate to each other in love. *Envy*, or malice, resents that someone else should enjoy a good we want for ourselves. It is a refusal to accept one's own finite gifts and to rejoice in those belonging to others. *Anger* is the desire to destroy whatever or whomever stands in the way of one's own self-seeking.

The final two go deepest of all, to the center of our relationship with God. *Accidie* is a Middle English word, retrieved because the usual word, "sloth," now only expresses a trivial laziness. Accidie is a form of spiritual despair, a refusal of grace, a bargain with nothingness that shuts out God's gift of the new possibility. The final sin, *pride*, is aggressively claiming one's self as the center of reality, displacing God and everyone else.

The rest of this book considers each "deadly sin" in turn. Rather than focusing on particular actions that are sinful or on the demonic power behind sin itself, I will try to open up the old vocabulary describing sinful dispositions in human character. Each chapter will spend some time praising God's good creation in the very area of life affected by the particular "deadly sin" being described. Then Scripture and contemporary experience will shed light onto the sin itself. Each chapter concludes with a section called "remedies": what God may do to heal each of these sins in us and our communities, and how we may respond. Thus we hope to learn to do what our world has been forgetting: how to speak of sin, in penitence and hope, and thereby to be alert to the terrible and glorious realities that surround us.

Chapter 2

Gluttony

S he has strong hands. Their fine lines are dusted by the flour her fingers are working in a bowl. As she swirls a slurry of yeast and warm water into it, she gathers the thickening stuff together, thumps and gropes and turns and stretches it with powerful fingers until the dough is an elastic ball. She drops it into a clean bowl and leaves it to itself. When she comes back two hours later, a pillow has risen. Slapped down flat and folded, it is still resilient to the touch. Soon it rises to fill the bowl again. She divides it, folds it, shapes it, puts it in pans, and leaves it again. Later she places the pale, puffy dough into the heat of the oven. When she reaches to take the pans out, the loaves glow brown and yellow and fill the room with their smell. She takes one to a table in the room. There, later, she will give thanks and then break it up to be eaten by hungry friends.

To the attentive mind, the creation of bread is itself a journey of wonders, from the earth to the oven: sun and water, soil and air becoming wheat, wheat ground into flour, flour transformed into bread. The material was worked by many hands before it reached the woman's: those of farmers, harvesters, grinders, merchants. Broken at her table, the bread undergoes an even more wonderful change. As people chew and swallow, the miracle of digestion transforms it into their own bodies, turning bread into human beings. More: the bread gathers them together as friends. If she brings the second loaf to another table in another house, among a wider company and with fuller thanksgiving, it will undergo a still greater metamorphosis. "Those who eat of this bread: they shall live forever." Every level of human existence—material, physical, economic, social, and divine—comes together in eating bread.

Elsewhere, a man in a straw hat walks along rows of vines that stretch out in straight lines for hundreds of yards before him in the staring heat. Stooping, he grasps the bunches of grapes, swollen and dusty, that hide under the leaves. Cutting them free, he tosses them into the basket on his back. In a few minutes, he runs the basket, heavy and full of scent in the hot air, back to the truck at the end of the row, and empties it. Soon full, the truck pulls away to the huge press. There the grapes are crushed and left to stand, now a foamy, aromatic stew, the yeast on the broken skins reacting with the grapes' liquid heart. Then, later, the liquid runs off into barrels. Lined up in dark rows, the barrels stand still. Months later, the taps are opened and ranks of bottles move down a line, filling with red liquid.

In a shop, another man buys two bottles and takes them away. A bottle is opened for his table at home. As the level in the bottle falls, the tongues of his friends are loosened in speech and song and thanks. When on Sunday he brings the other bottle to another house and another kind of table, much the same thing happens, though on an even deeper level and with higher words and songs. Out of soil and sun and water grapes have become wine through the work and skill of many people. That wine itself is transformed into human life, and at the Lord's table it conveys a life greater still.

All of creation comes together in bread and wine. In the most basic of human foods, divine and social and material existence are at one.

Of course it need not be so. Creation may be reversed and the process made to run backwards. The wine bottles may be emptied by one person alone, the drinker becoming a stew as shapeless as the contents of the fermenting vat. The loaves may be gobbled alone. If the drinker or the eater craves more, there is only the quick run to the corner store to repeat the process. Then the miracle of bread and wine, bond of all of life from the biochemical to the divine, is wasted in gluttony.

— The Sin of Gluttony —

Gluttony is a deadly sin. Gluttony is a reversal of creation, the spoiling and corruption of bread and wine and all that goes with them. Gluttony is eating and drinking that excludes God. Formally, it is a spiritual disease that feeds on our need for food and drink and for the other necessities of bodily life. Those needs, seated in the physical side of life, are good in themselves. When God kneaded together human life out of the dust of the ground and breathed his Spirit into it, physical needs were blessed. They are basic to human life. Hungry people need to eat and thirsty people need to drink because they cannot live if they do not.

Yet there is more than one way to eat and drink. Right eating brings health, and spreads it throughout the world. Wrong eating twists back upon itself, and spreads a void, a hunger that wastes life. A mystery can be lived so that it gives life. It can also be reversed and wasted.

There is something more at issue. "You are what you eat," a cynic wrote, with more truth than he knew. One of the strangest sides of eating is how much it has to do with human identity. Both what we eat and how we eat have a great deal to do with who we are. That is obviously true on the most basic level; if you cease to eat, you cease to be. But there are more subtle aspects—your food becomes who you are. It can change you, making you more yourself, or less. Purer water and better food have substantially increased the height and life span of Europeans in this century, but there is a malign side of the same principle. Some Japanese who, years ago, ate fish contaminated with mercury now have twisted bones and muscles. The poison still resides in them, is now part of them, misshaping them as they grow. Terribly, they are what they ate.

The principle is true in ways that go beyond the physical. Personal identity is shaped by our social life, and eating is social, shared. The stranger who is offered bread and salt by a desert nomad knows that he is not an alien any longer but known as a person in relationship with the one who offers the food. Families grow up around kitchen tables.

Even more deeply, you are what you eat before God. In almost every culture that grew out of the Old Testament (and in many others as well), eating and drinking have the capacity to be holy, actions that impinge on the divine. Jews will not eat unclean food, particularly any food that might have been offered to a false god, because they know that their eating and drinking identifies them as the true Israel, prepared for the priestly service of the one God.

You are what you eat. For that reason, gluttony is part of an old conspiracy to fabricate one's own identity by eating and drinking, to create and sustain oneself by turning the miracle of food and drink into self-creation and self-service, excluding God. That is sin, and with sin comes death. At the personal, individual level, gluttony is physically deadly: it may kill its victim through overeating or through poor nutrition. Corporately, gluttony can kill millions throughout the world, when gluttons keep all the bread for themselves and will not share it with the hungry. Yet psychically, socially, spiritually it is deadly, too. It destroys or corrupts the life of those who eat without thanks: who feed their own life while displacing God.

These will seem like unnecessarily deep waters to most Americans, who want little enough from life—only a calorie-free pizza. For most modern people, eating has no particular meaning. It is true that we are now learning to see the significance of food and drink in new ways. Anxieties about pesticides, a desire for what is pure and wholesome, growing awareness of the implications of our place at the top of the food chain, the study of diseased relationships to food and drink, from alcoholism to anorexia and bulimia, have all begun to evoke a response. Our schools try hard to teach children about nutrition. (Any teacher with a sense of self-preservation is bound to do so, after contending with a class of seven-year-olds demented by sugar.) At the same time the media bombard us with images of fast-food juxtaposed with images of the starving. More and more churches struggle to feed the hungry in our midst, and are obscurely aware of how deep the mystery is that they are acting out.

Yet as families scatter to fast-food outlets and single people shove individual portions of frozen suppers into the microwave, the social character of eating and drinking has become remote. In my neighborhood, only a minority of families regularly share any common meal. In particular, the notion that eating and drinking may be holy, a threshold to the divine, seems ludicrous. Who, confronted by a hospital vending machine full of refrigerated, cellophane-wrapped sandwiches, could consider eating to be sacred? Diet soda, sugarless candy, supermarket bread have all lost their connection with the soil of the earth and the life of God.

Most distant of all, perhaps, is the idea that eating and drinking could involve sin. That is not to say that guilt and shame do not cluster around eating. It is common for American women in particular to experience guilt and shame about any kind of pleasure in food, while guilt may paralyze people addicted to food or drink. Yet it does not occur to us to use the vocabulary of sin. In part that is for a good reason—today the meaning of sin has been so reduced that it refers only to actions freely and willingly performed by individuals who for some reason choose not to exercise "will power." In this context the sin of gluttony, meaning eating and drinking that excludes God, does not fit the reality of addiction. Yet not all sins are freely chosen and renounced simply by will power, and in the sense that addiction implies eating and drinking that exclude God, the word sin might fit the reality in a deeper way. Some Christians have thought that even the created order itself has been damaged by sin, so that food and wine, wholesome in themselves, might become addictive poison.

In gluttony the power of sin comes to focus on food and drink. There is a succession of stories of wrong eating in the Bible, from the fruit in the Garden of Eden, eaten so that the human pair might be "like God," to the morsel taken by Judas before he went out into the night to betray Jesus. Those stories go to the heart of what the Christian tradition means by sin. Those meals were eaten by human beings who wished to define their identities and purposes by displacing God. All human eating and drinking is implicated in those meals. But Scripture also offers us stories of right eating, from the manna in the wilderness to the Supper of the Lamb, stories that offer Christ's new possibility to all who hunger and thirst for it. Those stories are about God's miracle of forgiveness, freeing his people from slavery to sin to feed them in the wilderness and seat them at his table forever.

— The Staff of Life —

Blessed art thou, Lord our God, King of the universe, who bringest forth bread from the earth.

Blessed art thou, Lord our God, King of the universe, who createst the fruit of the vine.

With these simple words Jewish people bless God for the food and drink of life, as they have done for millennia. God is named "Blessed," with a blessedness that is immense and eternal, that humans live to know and worship. God shares that blessedness with us in sheer generosity. It weaves its way through daily life, in family and work, sunrise and sunset. All the foundations of human life are from God, who creates them and gives them—among them bread and wine, the staff of life. God has made all things, and made them good. Eating and drinking are part of the *shalom*, the life-giving peace of God. When we eat bread and drink wine with thanks, we are caught up in God's peace and blessing.

This sharing in God's blessedness is true in every part of life. When Christians offer bread and wine to God in the Lord's Supper, they are bringing the whole cosmic order to God, from the primal elements to their own full humanity, all caught up in the mystery of bread. When farmers grow wheat, physical matter (soil and seed, water and sunshine) comes together with human wisdom and labor. It takes a culture of yeast to make bread and a human culture to teach people how to use the yeast; biology and sociology come together at the baker's. The whole economic order brings bread to the table. All of that is offered to God in the bread. All of it is received back as the Body of Christ, the culmination of all God's blessings. Bread is a sign of the relationship with God himself, who is the real center of human life. Jesus calls himself the Bread of Life. God feeds us with himself, gives us the divine life that relationship with him implies.

When friends gather around a table to break bread, bodies are nourished, strengthened, satisfied. It is such a pleasure to eat good bread and wine, to smell and chew and taste. What spreads through the body also strengthens the soul. At the end of a day, often heartsick and tired, I go home. My body feels the effects of hunger, the aches and the low blood sugar that come from hard work without food. Those effects extend to the irritability and depression of my spirit. But my spirit, too, is pulled out of shape by the day's stresses and conflicts, and my body shares in that dislocation. The routine of getting dinner on the table draws me into its pattern. At dinner, bread and wine work their magic on a beaten body, giving me peace and well-being. Sitting down with people I love, to eat, to talk, restores me to my true self.

As a child I did whatever I could to avoid preparing supper or doing the dishes afterwards, but I loved the meal itself—the food, the talk, the faces and voices, the movement of word and glances across the table. Now I love it all, preparation and clean-up too, especially when the kitchen is shared with someone else. At supper my children and my wife teach me who I am. Friendships are much the same when knit together by a shared table, by broken bread and poured wine. It is hard for me to imagine how people could be friends without sharing a meal. Comrades share enthusiasm, colleagues arrive at a common vision around food and drink. Gluten knits a loaf together; bread at a common table binds human lives together. It is this miracle, reaching from God and returning to him, that gluttony breaks, shrinks, wastes.

— The Wasting Disease —

Jim is a respectable and decent government official. He has only one secret vice: little frosted chocolate cakes. Every day he buys four packages of them, eight little cakes in all, about twenty-four bites of pleasure for one working day. Each bite is a little burst of reward. Of course the joggers in his office would not approve; they are already contemptuous about his plump "self-presentation." So he keeps the little cakes in a bottom drawer of his desk, and eats them only when no one is around. His doctor is not very pleased with his weight, but who really cares? What harm is he doing?

Gluttony has not gotten very far with Jim yet; he only has a minor case. As Augustine of Hippo, the great North African theologian of the fifth century, taught Christians to see, there is quite a bit of good in the picture. The pleasure and comfort Jim obtains are good in themselves. Little chocolate cakes qualify for a share in God's *shalom*. But observe what the disease has done. The food Jim is eating is for pleasure and comfort only, not to minister to the health of his body. The nutrition contained in those cakes is negligible, "empty calories," making him fat without making him strong. That is to say, his eating does not really bless his body, only his sensuality. The same is true on the emotional level. Jim's sugar highs are followed by insulin lows that make his emotional weather unsettled and his body in constant need of more sugar. He eats the goodies repetitively, obsessively, without recognizing them as miracle. They are eaten furtively, alone. Most of all, they are eaten without thanksgiving. If Jim would stop and bless God over his little cakes before he ate them, he might not eat them at all.

This is not a portrait of a man drawn into God's blessing. God's gift of food and drink is not weaving Jim's life together into a whole. Rather, his life is fragmented. His body is separated from his sensuality. He eats apart from other people. He has no reason to remember or give thanks; he just unwraps, chews, and waits for the next cake. Sin fragments, alienates, shrinks human life.

This judgment may seem rather overwhelming to modest gluttons like most of us. When Jesus attacked the Pharisees, after all, it was not for overeating. Presumably Thomas Aquinas was not damned for the plate of herring he was eating when his heart gave up the weary task of pushing blood through his ox-like body. Yet even at such minor levels, gluttony may not be trivial.

Gluttony sets in when the part becomes the whole. When one eats for pleasure or comfort alone, what dominates the scene is the self. I want the pleasure or comfort for me. Other people, other realities (including God) are pushed to the periphery. Food and drink may quickly become the main means of pleasure in life, the chief source of comfort. The whole purpose of food to nourish life is pushed aside; what glutton eats for *nutrition?* Social life engages the glutton only as a means to get food. Who really wants to share? I remember once locking myself in the bathroom to eat a chocolate bar without interruption, with my two-year-old daughter hammering at the door demanding a bite.

Most of the time, early-stage gluttony only produces a certain spiritual sluggishness. Comforted, indulged, and self-satisfied, the modest glutton simply will not respond to God's word or God's mission with as much alertness or energy. But this road has a definite pitch, which may become much steeper. Cut off from other realities, the pleasures and comforts may wear thin quickly and need constant renewal. As the appetite is stimulated, it seeks more and more to sustain the old level of comfort. The rewards themselves create hunger; the hunger seeks greater rewards. In this spiral looms obsession, the growth of appetite less and less connected to any other reality, less and less satisfied by the very pleasures it seeks.

That usually brings with it a need for control. To keep the rewards coming, one must provide carefully for a constant supply. Security becomes a well-packed refrigerator or liquor cabinet, a sort of instant cash machine for pleasure. But maintaining that supply takes attention and foresight and the use of either manipulation or domination of the world outside. One glutton may do this by wheedling, another by conquering; but the rewards must keep coming. The glutton seems to be in control, indeed, to control everything where food is concerned, but at the center is a hunger that controls the glutton.

As gluttony ceases to be simply a disposition of one's character and becomes demonic, freedom of heart and mind is lost. In food-related disorders like anorexia and bulimia, victims are digested by their own appetites. Struggling to control their world, they are obsessed by thoughts of food and violent hunger. Desperately searching for a self, they are repelled by the vision of themselves as evil, fat, ugly. They starve or gorge and vomit. The final outcome of full-grown sin is death: in this case, literal physical death. But every level of life dies. God, family, work, all wholesome pleasure are destroyed bit by bit by the victim's thirst or hunger. The addict's own self crumbles, crippled by resentments and fears. For them, little exists except the obsession.

The desire for power is also part of gluttony. On the most trivial level, anyone who has ever tried to make a three-year-old eat zucchini is aware how easily a family dinner can turn into a power struggle. One can eat for power, force-feed for power, starve another for power. The agricultural and trade policies of many countries, including our own, serve ends far removed from feeding the hungry. As I write these words, two regimes in Ethiopia are using starvation as a crucial weapon in their fight to control that hungry land, one side displacing farmers and the other destroying food convoys. And how much of the insight, effort, and innovation of which Americans are capable has gone into the effort to feed those who starve and to help them feed themselves? Into spreading the *shalom* of God to those less fortunate? Loving our own purposes and our own power too well, we sit tight, governing our pantries for ourselves. Our gluttony creates a world that exists to serve our own appetites to the exclusion of others and of God, and this also is what Christians call sin.

— Living by Bread Alone —

The greatest danger of gluttony is its core of self-idolatry. "You are what you eat." From the beginning, people have hoped that they could find a food that would make them gods.

Immediately after his baptism in the Jordan, after the Spirit descended on him and God declared him to be his beloved Son, Jesus was put to the test: forty days of hunger.

> The tempter came and said to him, "If you are the Son of God, command these stones to become loaves of bread." But he answered, "It is written, 'One does not live by bread alone, but by every word that comes from the mouth of God.'" (Matt. 4:3-4)

As always, hunger brought with it the most basic questions. If you are starving, then your personal existence is at stake. The tempter drove those questions home. Prove who you are by using your power to feed your hunger! Who are you really? Who controls the shape of your life, and directs your creative powers?

Jesus' forty days of fasting echoed the long hunger of his people, Israel's forty years in the desert. Long before, Moses had explained to Israel what God's purpose was in giving them nothing to eat but manna as he led them from slavery to the promised land:

> Remember the long way that the Lord your God has led you these forty years in the wilderness....He humbled you by letting you hunger, then by feeding you with manna, with which neither you nor your ancestors were acquainted, in order to make you understand that one does not live by bread alone, but by every word that comes from the mouth of the Lord. (Deut. 8:2-3)

Israel had learned to accept a false identity as slave of Pharaoh. If they were dominated by harsh masters, at least everything was under control. Meals were regular and reliable, with garlic and leeks to spice them up. All that familiar world ended at the Red Sea. God called them into a freedom defined by him only, dependent on him only. For forty years Israel was led by God in the desert, always one day away from hunger. Their hunger posed a choice. It could send them back to the garlic and leeks of Egypt to build more temples for idols, or force them to unlearn the idolatry still in their hearts.

The same choice faced Jesus in the desert. When the tempter found Jesus there, hungry, he drove straight to the heart of the matter. What the devil proposed was the archetypical act of gluttony: *"If* you are the Son of God, turn these stones into loaves." *"If* you are the Son of God"—at stake was Jesus' basic identity. *"Turn* these stones into bread"—what came with it was the question of control. How Jesus related to bread went to the heart of who he was and who would shape his life.

In response, Jesus quoted Moses: "One does not live by bread alone, but by every word that comes from the mouth of God." Starvation might threaten Jesus' bodily life, but even so he knew that his life and identity depended simply on God. To be Son of God was more a matter of God's word than of bread. He would not make his Father prove that word to be true by trying out his own powers on some stones. That would not be faithful dependence, but rather a self-defining act of controlling power. He would be asserting himself as God's rival, not God's Son. But Jesus was who he was by his Father's continuous begetting. His life was shaped by his Father's call to his Father's mission.

Nowhere does Matthew suggest that Jesus did not need bread, or that it was wrong for him to be hungry and to want bread badly. Human life depends on bread, but not on bread eaten apart from God. Gluttony, however, means to live by bread alone.

When Jesus declined the devil's invitation to dine, he reversed a long tradition. Eve and Adam had seized the fruit the serpent offered so as to make themselves "like God," rather than living by the word of God. Esau sold his future in God's promise for a "mess of pottage." Israel in the desert craved the leeks and garlic of Egypt, and complained bitterly about the manna. Leviticus listed hundreds of unclean foods that would leave Israelites unable to approach God in priestly worship. Even in the New Covenant, Judas' last meal carried on the same tradition. Wrong eating is still possible at the very central act of the church's life. The Lord's Supper, Paul tells us, is a meal that brings death to those who eat "without discerning the body" (1 Cor. 11:29). That Bread, like all bread, brings life if eaten one way, in faith and thanksgiving; but eaten in another way, in gluttony, it will kill.

— Remedies —

Under the shadow of his own death Jesus ate the Passover meal with his friends. That bread and wine, fruits of the field and the vineyard, had long been signs of the harvest of all things in God's kingdom. But Jesus went further. He named them his body and his blood. His body was going to be broken on the cross, his blood poured out, leaving his identity and purpose utterly in his Father's hands. Thus the bread and the wine of Jesus' last supper became a primary means by which the resurrection would break through to his disciples. Jesus gave himself to be eaten and drunk, to enter every part of human existence in forgiveness, in new identity, in mission. The people at that table could eat and become one with him; thus they were free to offer all their life to God. Who they would be, how their life would be shaped was to be defined by what they ate at that meal: Christ's Body.

The Eucharist is that same meal and it has the same effects. Remedies for gluttony begin there. One sets aside all other food and drink for that bread and wine; there one's hungers are redirected true and straight, to Christ. Healing for the body and the promise of its resurrection may be found there, the deepest nutrition. The mind and heart are refreshed in ways they can begin to understand and in many they cannot. Around the table one finds sisters and brothers, friends in a family that is not born of any blood but Jesus'. That table stretches out invisibly through all time, from beginning to end, to all peoples, assembling "his body, the fullness of him who fills all in all" (Eph. 1:23). You are what you eat; so God feeds us with himself.

It is in the strength of that food that Christians can begin to appreciate hunger rightly. Israel learned to live by the word of God only through forty years of eating nothing but a daily ration of manna. Jesus' sonship came to a point during his forty days of hunger. Hunger is crucial. There are other foods we crave that we must not eat, and ways of eating we must unlearn. There are hungers that have to grow sharper if our other hungers are to give way to them. It was once the universal custom that one came to the feast of the Eucharist only after fasting from all lesser foods. Christian gluttons need to learn how to be hungry for God. For that reason, Christians must fast.

Christian fasting is little practiced these days, and even less understood. Some consider fasting just another disguise for hostility to the human body. The opposite is true. Because body and spirit are one, what happens to the body matters a great deal to the spirit. Christian fasting is primarily a matter of learning to live, not by bread alone, but by God's word. Well-fed slaves in a land far from God must learn concretely, physically, to depend on God: to be who it is God means them to be, to live in a world shaped by God's will. God's will must be set first, not only in theory but in the very rhythms of the body. That relearning, that letting go of our grasp so as to be grasped by God, is the point of fasting—a small share in Jesus' cross.

Perhaps food and drink have been your chief comfort and chief pleasure, and you are fat. Perhaps they seem nasty and distasteful, and you are thin. Perhaps food has chiefly been a means of sexual or economic power. Then Christian fasting means learning honest hunger and thankful eating, in which the words that come from the mouth of God take on a fresh significance for life, and bread and wine do too.

Many people need to fast, in the literal sense of a disciplined and prayerful abstention from food, as one part of a life of Christian discipline. To turn away from old tangles in sensuality, fasting helps. To learn to love justice more than one's own comfort, fasting helps. To give up autonomy and learn dependence on God, fasting helps. To live into God's future, giving up our tight grip on today, fasting helps. In particular, Christians of the First World, powerful, wealthy, and replete with every luxury, need to learn to fast again and find out what it means to hunger and thirst after justice.

There are, of course, dangers. Fasting itself can be diseased, punitive, damaging. Worse, it is possible to fast so as to extend one's own power over self and the world, rather than to turn to God. There have been many cases in which fasting focused one's own personal power for the sake of domination. Rasputin fasted in order to corrupt and manipulate the Tsar's family. Medieval handbooks for spiritual directors echoed Jesus' warning against fasting for religious prestige. That is why one must fast with Christ, alert for the tempter. In my own church's tradition, most fasting occurs at specific times of the Christian year, when the whole community fasts together. The forty days of Lent correspond to Jesus' forty days and Israel's forty years of hunger in the desert. Lent follows the long road leading to Jesus' cross and resurrection, which is the end of all Christian fasting. It leads to Easter, when, free in body and heart, Christians can feast on the Bread of Heaven, their true being as God's daughters and sons restored, the hope of God's kingdom renewed.

That leads to a second remedy for gluttony: thanksgiving. The Great Thanksgiving of the Easter Eucharist must extend to every meal that Christians eat, every table where they gather. One must give thanks over food, whenever and wherever one eats—preeminently at the Lord's table, but even when eating a little chocolate cake at one's desk. To give thanks to God for our food means recollecting what we are doing when we eat, and rejoicing in our dependence on God as we receive all that astounding miracle of creation from him. People who give thanks for their food cannot push other people away, as if the food were their own creation for themselves. Thanksgiving will draw them into mission: to alter this world so that the hungry can be fed, and justice done; to share the Bread of Heaven with the millions around us who have never tasted him, and do not yet know that he is good.

Chapter 3

Lust

One summer during the doldrums of August, it came time for me to tell my son the "facts of life." At any rate that was my wife's view. She had introduced our two older daughters to the birds and the bees without my help, and she considered it my business to tell Michael. I tried to help her see that her attitude was unenlightened, but when that failed I unmoored myself from the couch and hove on down to the local children's bookstore to arm myself with literature. Fully equipped, I returned home to think it through. On one hand there was the biology of the whole thing to be conveyed to a nine-year-old. Gametes are strange enough, let alone the implausible event that brings the gametes together. Then there was the whole matter of human relationship as male and female, of love, of birth, of family; the great fields of ethics and spirituality stretching out beyond; and Michael's and my own relationship, as son and father. Sides of the thing, all so different from each other, and yet all one—how could I help him see the whole mystery coming together in unity?

I realized there was no question of my *introducing* Michael to the mystery of sexuality, because he was in the midst of it already. Passionate parents; older sisters; one godfather a celibate monk, other godparents a long-married couple; several gay cousins; divorce among friends at school and church;

exposure to the sexual avalanche of the media—he had been finding his way within the mystery ever since he was born. Even before his birth, the mystery had enclosed him in his mother's flesh. Yet there awaited many more initiations, births of a sort, entries into new worlds, of which this particular step, talking with his fumbling father, was only one.

How complex it all is! Things that seem utterly different to modern people, from biology to sacramental theology, come together in sex. The intense physical pleasure of climax is different in kind, one might think, from the deep communion between a woman and a man who have been married fifty years, or from the passionate prayer of a contemplative drawn beyond words into Christ. God has no trouble in holding such goods together, but we do. Our world tends to divide what God has joined together; confused, we cannot grasp the whole. During one day we move from having a pap smear to watching Marilyn Monroe in *Some Like It Hot* to visiting our parents. Add to this fragmentation the fact that sin plays its own merry hell with the goodness of sex, and the result is complex badness woven through complex goodness: lust corrupting, and yet never wholly destroying, the gift of sexual love.

Christians have never fully agreed, and still don't, on quite how to make sense of sex. Not surprisingly, lust—the name of the deadly sin that attacks the gift of sex—has been understood in quite distinct ways. The complex reality of human sexuality has received a complex response from Christians.

What virtually all Christians have agreed on, until quite recently, was a certain basic moral grammar for sexual behavior. Christians have always honored celibacy, at least in theory. They have always honored marriage, at least in theory. And they have always prohibited a list of sexual actions, including such acts as adultery and fornication. The lists varied somewhat among different communities, but they could all be summarized as prohibiting any form of sexual intercourse outside of marriage.[*] Today many Christians question some of those basic rules because they find them harsh, stifling, or unworthy of a Gospel in which love has replaced law. I myself accept them as a fixed point of Christian tradition, rooted in Scripture and revealed through two millennia of common life as guardians of love.

Even so, these are simple rules of moral grammar, not coherent teachings about the gift of sexuality and how lust invades it. If Christians at one time all agreed on the rules, there was no such agreement about a theological rationale for them. A quick look at a few approaches to understanding lust that have come and gone throughout our history might help illustrate the point.

Some Christians have treasured the basic rules as guardians of the holiness and purity of the life of the eucharistic community. From this point of view, lust is a force of anarchy and pollution. Celibacy and marriage are holy, unambiguously blessed by God; they explicitly model God's kingdom. Thus they support the church's consecration to God. But other sexual acts ignore God's holiness, in this tradition's view, creating unions that pollute the communion of God's people with God and each other. Paul argues that whoever has sexual intercourse with a prostitute enters a personal communion that in turn infects the church's communion with Christ (1 Cor. 6:15ff.). From this perspective, lust is a lawless sacramentalism that compromises the community's intimacy with a holy God.

The trouble with this approach, if taken too far, is that Jesus clearly taught that the holiness of God's community depended on God's own holiness, triumphant and self-giving,

---

[*] See my article, "Sexual Norms in the Medieval Church," in *A Wholesome Example,* ed. Robert W. Prichard (Lexington, KY: Bristol Books, 1993), 35-44.

not on his people's avoidance of polluting behavior. Further, Jesus attacked external purity laws that did not serve an inner purity of heart, inviting into his community anyone who knew they needed God, including prostitutes. In the church, sexual purity has sometimes been enforced in cruel and hypocritical ways. Homosexuals have been banned from churches; unmarried women who became pregnant have been shamed and excluded; at times menstruating women have been kept from the Lord's table, not to mention the priesthood. This understanding of lust can degenerate into the heresy that sees all sex as a pollutant in spite of the clear teaching in Genesis that God created sex and called it good.

It is wrong to reject this view of lust entirely, however. The spate of complaints about sexual exploitation by clergy makes that clear. A priest who has sex with parishioners and then celebrates the Eucharist with them does indeed pollute their communion with Christ. Again and again I have seen the infection: lost faith, distorted experience, demonic secrets all smelling of their source. My friend Lois's weekly agony, when she makes her communion near the woman who seduced her husband, shows that lust can introduce Satan into the church's very heart.

Another approach to lust came into clear focus during the ascetical movement in the fourth century, when thousands of men and women went into the desert seeking freedom of heart so as to know God directly. For them, lust expressed two related evils. It was one of the "passions"—self-destructive habits of heart—by which demonic powers enslaved people. At the same time, it distracted contemplatives from concentration on God. The issue here is not so much the way that lust violates the community's holiness, but its role in the inner life of the individual. Lust rules people's hearts instead of God, and pulls them constantly away from deepening attention to God.

The danger of this approach, of course, is that it can lead people to consider any sexual feelings as evil, and to cultivate a rejecting sexlessness of character as divine. On the contrary: passionate and faithful sexual love can lead people into intense moments of praise and worship of God. Yet sexual lust can easily become obsessive, self-seeking, addictive. It can serve as a distraction, not just from contemplation of God, but from any relationship or duty. One of the most celebrated and often-told medieval love poems was of Tristan and Isolde, whose passion burned away their vows to their spouses, their loyalty to subjects and liege-lords, their word, their souls.

A third approach, perhaps the best known, received its classical statement by scholastic theologians such as Thomas Aquinas. Influenced by the philosopher Aristotle's belief that human conduct should have a purpose and should seek some good that the mind could grasp, these theologians defined lust as "inordinate desire"—a desire not shaped by its proper purposes. The natural desire of people to copulate should be directed by a comprehensive vision of what they are made for. Sex has a purpose, so the argument went, and that purpose includes the getting and raising of children. But that goal itself must be set in the larger perspective of the society in which those children will seek to build a humane life, and of the church in which they will seek to come into union with God. Sexual acts motivated by nothing more than a spasm of need or a personal obsession—lust—ignore the other dimensions of human life. Lust is "inordinate" because it is not ordered by that vision of larger meaning; lust is blind. Thus inevitably it is dysfunctional: personally, socially, and spiritually destructive.

This third approach to lust has its dangers, too: an excessive rationality. Generations of Christians have thought that, even in the marriage bed, they had somehow to keep at the forefront of their minds a deliberate, clear-headed intention to have a baby, never getting silly and having fun together. At the same time, the fragmenting and manipulative use of sexual images by the advertising media shows how vulnerable to distortion sex can be when it has no coherent purpose.

There have been many approaches to lust besides these. They do not necessarily exclude each other, but they differ. Each has its own particular revealing and helpful side; each has its limitations; any of them may pose serious dangers. Instead of following any one of them exclusively, I would like to push a little deeper into a specific dimension of sin that is clearly revealed by the sin of lust: that sin is everywhere. No part of our sexual lives is wholly good, short of heaven; no part is wholly evil, short of hell. Evil is woven together with all the goods of human life. Thus sexual life is ambiguous: much good to praise, much evil to mourn. Even when we aim for the good, we miss the mark. Which is why every day God greets us with inexhaustible tenderness and forgiveness.

One of the Greek words for sin used repeatedly in the New Testament is *hamartia*. It literally means, "missing the mark." The image is from archery. Whether one is shooting at targets for sport or hunting game for food or waging war, one shoots to hit the mark. *Hamartia* is when you miss. Missing matters; a miss is as good as a mile when a missed target on the battlefield will shoot back, or when one must come home from the field without supper. Yet in target practice, there is a great difference between barely missing the bullseye and wounding the instructor standing ten yards away. In some contexts, *hamartia* underlines the either/or character of spiritual life; either one meets the standard, or one misses it. Yet in other contexts one can value the near misses, the partial goodness of some failures.

God sets the mark for human life, sex included. Indeed, one could say that God *is* the mark. From this perspective, it is easy to see why Scripture says that "all have sinned and come short of the glory of God." Some aim well; some aim badly; all miss the mark. Yet Scripture also says that God has included all in sin, so that he might include all in mercy. In sexual matters, everyone misses the mark one way or another; that is the despair of sin, its helplessness, its universality. And to recognize that is to be prepared for the sheer gift, offered equally to all whether they miss the mark by an inch or a mile: God's forgiveness in Jesus.

— Aiming at the Mark —

When I am standing before a man and a woman to bless their marriage, I have the best view in the house. The beauty and uniqueness of every woman and every man are embodied in these two people. The solemn entry of the man from one side and the woman from the other enacts their coming together. They turn to each other, join eyes, join hands. They *see* each other, looking toward a lifelong knowing of the one they have chosen to love. They *hold* each other, physically linked. When they take their vows, joining their hands, that holding defines them from that day forward—in sickness and in health, in wealth and poverty, in good times and bad. The invocation of the Trinity in the celebration of a marriage is not incidental; it is God's blessing they seek, the God in whose image they are created. God is One, as they wish to become one in their own way. God is also three distinct persons in communion, as they wish to be two distinct persons in communion.

It is not good for a man to be alone. The story of our first creation in Genesis still places sexual love at the heart of creation. In Paradise, Adam and Eve were given to each other to know and love. They were clearly different from each other; the glory one glimpses in the beloved is not one's own. Yet they were both human, consubstantial, and in rejoined bodies they became one flesh. As the story is told, only the creation of man and woman answered the primal human's longing for this sort of relationship. The animals shared bodily life with humans, but they did not know the transcendent God and were not in his image. Humans can love and rule animals, but not know and honor them with all they are and have. On the other side, God was not yet close enough to humans to be a companion, since the Word had not yet taken flesh. Erotic love in Paradise was both physical like animals' and ensouled like God's, difference finding mutual knowledge and love, and thus communion.

I do not know a man. The story of our race's second beginning, told by Luke, is of an angel visiting a virgin, announcing that she will be with child by the Holy Spirit. Our imaginations can no longer recognize the story as erotic, although in a different way from that of Eden. The One who knows and loves Mary is God. The Word she herself believes and loves, and thus receives into her flesh, is God. Finally, the Other for whom humans long is God. Mary comes into a new quality of union with the God who in her womb becomes flesh. Anyone can be united with Jesus' body, like Mary, and thus be made one flesh with God. Being held by and holding God; knowing and honoring God with all we have and are, as God knows and honors us: that is the endless marriage of which Eden's was only a sign. Outside of Eden, not all are called to human marriage. Yet the marriage of the Incarnation is one to which everyone is called, the Beloved who seeks everyone and who is the end of all seeking.

God's love, of course, is not confined to the erotic, nor is human life. Love has other forms and metaphors—parents and children, brothers and sisters, friends, colleagues, neighbors—all have their own sorts of love. As with all of these, erotic love aims at the common mark: the love of God.

> Hear what our Lord Jesus Christ saith: Thou shalt love the Lord thy God with all thy heart, and with all thy soul, and with all thy mind. This is the first and great commandment.

And the second is like unto it: Thou shalt love thy neighbor
as thyself. On these two commandments hang all the Law
and the Prophets.

God is love. The mark that God sets for human life to meet is
exactly that: love. Since human beings are made in God's image, we are expected to be and to act like him. That means
that God's love is the standard for sexual love, too. But what
sort of love? Not everything called love is like God's.

Israel's exodus with God helps to set the mark for human
love more clearly. In the panorama of gods worshiped in
Egypt, only one God heard the slaves' cry for justice and
came in love to free them. God's love is rooted in justice.
God's love makes others free. That is the mark for sexual love
as well. Absalom Jones, the first African American Episcopal
priest, aimed at it in his marriage. He worked day and night
for years to buy his wife's freedom from her "master." His
love for her bought her justice and freedom, at the price of
years of sweat and blood. Sexual love shaped like God's love
seeks the fullest life for the beloved.

God led his people through the desert to the mountain,
where they took each other in a covenant of love. The first
term of that covenant was, "You shall have no other gods but
me." God's union with Israel brooks no rivals. That "jealousy," that exclusiveness, is not arbitrary, but is grounded in
reality. There is only one God, and worship belongs to him
only. By the time of Jesus' birth, Israel had learned that les-
son. They had given up worshiping the sexual force as god,
although most of their neighbors did. Nor did they deify
their spouses, as if marriage were the final end of human life.
The marriages they did celebrate, however, were exclusive.
God's love modelled that: "You only have I known out of all
the nations of the earth." In great pain they had learned to
stop committing the "adultery" of worshiping the many idols
of the nations. Consequently, one woman and one man came

together in marriage, forsaking all others. Sexual love like God's is, in that sense, exclusive.

In the desert and beyond, God's love for Israel was faithful. He kept covenant, and he promised to do so forever. God's *hesed*, his faithfulness, his "constant sure love" that keeps promises forever, came to be mirrored in marriage. God's love is not trivial or temporary; it is committed and sure. For all of my life, I have had the rare privilege to be surrounded by people who struggled to keep their word in marriage and in celebacy. God's perseverance in love is the standard for ours, and human perseverance in our relationships of love teaches us about God's faithfulness. God keeps his vows. Given the profound changes in Israel's life, the terrible times of disobedience and ruptured relationship, God's faithfulness was tested to the core. But there was no final divorce. His love is everlasting.

God's love is life-giving, too. Israel learned that the whole world was God's good creation, filled with his love. The Psalms sing not only with thanksgiving for the gift of life, but also for the sheer joy of knowing and loving the God who is life.

> O Lord, how manifold are your works!
>> in wisdom you have made them all;
>> the earth is full of your creatures....
> All of them look to you
>> to give them their food in due season.
> You give it to them; they gather it;
>> you open your hand, and they are filled
>> with good things....
> You send forth your Spirit, and they are created;
>> and so you renew the face of the earth....
> I will sing to the Lord as long as I live;
>> I will praise my God while I have my being.

May these words of mine please him;
I will rejoice in the Lord. (Psalm 104)

Sexual love, like God's, is filled with life, with the power and joy of creation, with the daily renewal of delight in the beloved. That, in turn, gives rise to hospitality of spirit, to bearing children of the body and of the heart.

— Lust: Missing the Mark —

A familiar fantasy from sitcoms, soaps, romance novels, detective thrillers:

Fred has had his eye on Heidi for some weeks. She is fine-looking, moves through the office with sensual grace, laughs naturally. Heidi has noticed Fred's attention, and it's all right with her. She likes the bones of Fred's square face, his eyes, the fact that he's funny and easy-going. One day he is complaining about having to go back to his apartment to another frozen dinner, and she suggests that he come around to her place. He does. They eat, they talk, they draw close, they kiss, they make love. They speak kind words to each other, make the languid visit to the bathroom, feeling the body's and mind's separate memories of pleasure. At the door: thanks; see you at work tomorrow.

What harm? Two people got together for an evening, gave and took some pleasure; in a lonely world, that's good. There was at least a little mutual knowledge, some mutual respect, some giving and receiving. That, and the pleasure itself, are blessings. Why call it sin, and look for lust?

Heidi and Fred broke a small but basic rule of Christian moral grammar, by having intercourse without marriage. Since I consider the rule as God's, breaking it is to me at least a provisional sign that they missed the mark. But such rules cannot by themselves reveal much about the potential and the inner character of what people do. Can any of the understandings of lust we have already explored shed any light?

The first view sees lust as idolatrous anarchy, compromising the consecration of the church to God alone. Fred and Heidi hardly saw their one-night stand as bringing something demonic or polluted into their relationship with God. Happily, they were a thousand miles from the heresy that views all sex as essentially ugly. But in point of fact they were a thousand miles from thinking any sort of divine thought. The communion of their bodies did not mean to invite a deeper divine communion. If they introduced any pollution, it was simply that of godlessness. God was absent from their sexual life, and so in offering themselves at the Eucharist they would be offering a vacuum. On the other hand, nothing would keep either of them from taking some new person to bed the next night. That human pattern mirrors the pattern of idolatry: worshiping one god after another, for what one can get. That might have its own effects on the consecration of God's people to him alone.

The second view sees lust as passion: an addictive, enslaving habit of heart that opposes God's will and distracts us from God's presence. One would have a hard time seeing Heidi and Fred's desire to spend the night together as obsessive and enslaving. Yet their desire did not bring them toward God's kingdom, but instead continued a pattern of disconnection and indifference.

The third view, lust seen as inordinate desire, seems to fit the circumstances better. Certainly their desire was strong—they wanted each other and they took each other—but they did not mean for it to interfere with more important things. There was no violence or discourtesy; no laws were broken. Yet the sex was private and trivial, almost pointless. It was not ordered toward a greater vision of the good, either of social good—creating an enduring family or of raising children to know God and serve neighbor—or of a more private good, self-giving devotion to one other person.

If one is to see where Heidi and Fred missed the mark, it is clearer when the mark is set by God's love. They did nothing, small or great, for or against, each other's justice or freedom. They made no promise of exclusivity, giving no sign of God's oneness. Though they might see each other again, the enduring, faithful, committed character of God's love was not really on the horizon. Although their evening together was pleasant, it gave little life, compared with the generosity and creativity of God's love. Fred and Heidi did not aim at anything deliberately evil. Yet the mark for human life is set by our creation in God's image and likeness, and their evening fell well short of that mark. That is *hamartia:* sin.

Here is another case.

Phil has a special cabinet for his collection of videos and magazines. The older ones are just Playboys, *reasonably titillating photographs of bodies. More recently, however, he has ranged more widely. After work he selects what he wants: a lingerie video, if he is fairly relaxed. But sometimes he wants strong sex, something to occupy his anger as well as rouse his imagination. There is one video of women whipping each other that never fails. He has a drink, watches, masturbates. An hour or two in his special cabinet washes fear and disappointment out of the day; it draws him back again and again.*

In Phil's case, the power of lust is clearer. One could argue, of course, that he does not literally break the simple traditional rules. Watching pornographic videos cannot be found on any traditional list of prohibited acts; those lists were born in days when most Christians were poor and pornography rare and expensive. Its universal availability is a dubious miracle of modern technology. Still, one need not doubt that if the fathers and mothers of the church had known about it, they would have ruled it out.

It is not hard to see Phil's lust as polluting, particularly his sexual excitement at violence and degradation. The images infect his imagination, and his imagination does not stay put in his special cabinet. Instead, all of his relationships are affected: perhaps he mentally undresses the people he works with; perhaps he tries not to think of them at all, since they do not blend well with his fantasies. If his mother gets him to go to church when he visits, the devil enjoys bringing out those images at the altar rail. They are not capable of consecration.

Nor is it hard tó see this lust as enslaving passion. Phil is alone, but not free. He buys the fantasies that suit him, and depends on no one; sheer autonomy, one would think. Yet those fantasies form him, shape his appetites, lead him on. Before long, he needs new images, stronger ones. Like a person walking up a sand dune, there is nothing substantial in them to sustain his being. His foot slips through the sand and he has gotten no further, but is still climbing obsessively. His imagination is full of addictive images, scarcely real at all; there is no question of trying to contemplate God, or anything else.

His lust is "inordinate"—wholly without purpose, scarcely even the purpose of pleasure. The images insist on their own fragments: buttocks and penis, mouth and thighs. There is no attraction in larger visions, even of the human beings acting out these roles, let alone a vision for human life in common. Phil's lust is entirely interior to himself; it does not contribute to the building of a world for others. Greedily sucking the images he buys, there is no space for any other seeing or intending.

In Phil's lust, love is practically extinguished except for a residual narcissism. God's love creates a real world of living beings not himself; erotic love desires a true Other to unite with. Phil's lust has only the most remote connection with anything outside of himself: he lusts for ink dots on paper, and magnetic patterns in celluloid, for fantasies existing only in his own mind. Far from seeking justice and freedom for the Other whom he loves, he has no other. In the real world he ignores, the women and children who are the actors in his pornographic fantasies are often caught in cycles of addiction or exploitation. His lust is exclusive enough: he is alone. It is faithful enough: to his obsession. But it is absolutely sterile.

If one compared Phil's case to Heidi and Fred's, he has missed the mark far more widely than they. At least they had each other, in mutual pleasure and respect, for an evening. Phil has almost nothing. Lust's promises are empty.

Another case.

Jeff is a middle-aged, middle-class man who has been married for some years. Small grievances with his wife have mounted, and boredom has spread slowly like mold in a refrigerator. Yet he basically likes his life and his wife is part of his lifestyle. His marriage is tolerable, even important to him. He treats his wife well, is reasonably faithful.

On a business trip, however, he meets an attractive associate. After dinner in the hotel, they return to her room. She is sexually hungrier and has a different technique from his wife. It is exciting, lively, and no one gets hurt; no question of domination or financial exploitation or disease. They go their separate ways, Jeff back to his home and wife and normal persona. He may feel some dissonance, even guilt, as he remembers the other body while in bed with his wife that night, but he will not feel like a monster of lust, not in the twentieth century. Perhaps he is a bit guilty for "cheating," but he deserves his pleasures. The whole trivial affair took place in an entirely different context from his home life. He can easily put it out of his mind. Perhaps it will even liven up the marriage.

Jeff's adultery obviously misses the mark of God's love. He has not kept himself only to his wife; he is manifestly unfaithful to the promises of covenant. But perhaps the most obvious symptom of the disease of lust is the banality of the whole affair, and it points to the way that lust invites other, worse sins to invade. Lust acts in Jeff by disconnecting and alienating his sexual behavior from the rest of his life. It has no real significance for him or for anything else. It will be broken off from life, a deed of roughly the same importance as failing to brush his teeth one night.

How has this feat of trivialization been accomplished? Jeff has done it by creating a little separate world for himself on business trips, and a special self for that world. Away from home, he is a different man, and different standards apply— godlike power. The fact that he has broken his commitment in marriage is disguised by an intentional fragmentation of his life.

Jeff, of course, may see it as life-enhancing. His wife and his home are important to him, we said. Look closely: it is his needs and his life and his ego that count. One incentive to divide one's life into compartments is the vivid, secret pleasure of being the only one who knows all of them, the one who arranges them and manipulates them for one's self alone. How much like God that feels! But to stay in control, Jeff has divided his own persona: he is not the same person at home and on the road. In fact, however, that is not like God. God is "I am who I am," simply himself, wholly present wherever he is.

Thus it is that Jeff's lust carries with it an even more serious spiritual disease: that of pride. In the field of sexual life, he himself has displaced God. So it is with all the other deadly sins, which often wash up in the wake of lust. Avarice can accumulate "sex objects" as personal possessions, while anger can use sex to dominate or batter or avenge. Envy can sprout out of unappeased sexual longing, when someone else wins the love you crave. Accidie—sloth, despair—can demoralize us into being someone else's toy. For all those stronger liquors, lust makes a fine mixer. The mark at which we aim, love like God's, loving God and loving neighbor, seems far away.

Jesus' own teaching offered very little comfort for those who wished to escape indictment for lust.

> "You have heard that it was said, 'Do not commit adultery.' But I say to you that everyone who looks at a woman with lust has already committed adultery with her in his heart. If your right eye causes you to sin, tear it out and throw it away; it is better for you to lose one of your members than for your whole body to be thrown into hell." (Matt. 5:27-29)

It is not only people who overtly commit lustful acts who miss the mark, but even those who keep them covert, hidden within. If the mark we aim at is Jesus' own radical dedication to God, with nothing whatever, inner or outer, compromising it, then we all miss the mark. Lust compromises the communion of a spiritual director who falls in love with her directee, even if they do nothing about it. Passion pulls my eye to the marvelous bodies living it up in beer commercials on TV, granting me temporary citizenship in a kingdom not God's. Inordinate desire produces low grades in high school, when boyfriends supplant books. Similarly, one can remain physically exclusive to one's spouse but toy with delicious fantasies about others. One can remain faithful to vows to marriage or celibacy, but resent it. These are not great crimes of lust; they do not miss the mark by much—except the mark of loving as God loves, wholly. Thus lust reveals us as sinners, and sin as pervading our lives. *Hamartia:* we miss the mark.

— Remedies —

The people who gather for the Eucharist at my parish are decent respectable folk, few easily identified as monsters of lust. When at the beginning the celebrant proclaims the Summary of the Law, the two great commandments of love on which, Jesus said, hang all the Law and the Prophets, it usually goes by quickly, and we do not take much notice. Yet God has set the mark. Everyone there misses that mark of perfect love, one way or another. Many of us are divorced. A few are quietly "living together," heterosexual and homosexual. Some covet their neighbor's husband or wife. Others are in faithful marriages—faithful, until measured by God's faithfulness. Others are single and struggling to abstain, in spite of occasionally rebellious hearts; still others think there is no reason to struggle. Some are consecrated as celibates, but sometimes feel that loving Christ solely is too dull to be borne. All of us gather together; not all of us admit that we miss the mark, but we all do.

For centuries my church's liturgies all contained a general confession of sin, for the whole congregation. Everyone, we assumed, came to God daily having missed the mark, and needed to own it. We no longer keep that discipline at every service, but when we do, we speak clearly:

> Most merciful God, we confess that we have sinned against you in thought, word, and deed, by what we have done, and by what we have left undone. We have not loved you with our whole heart; we have not loved our neighbors as ourselves.

The confession is global: corporate and individual, inner heart and outer act, commission and omission. By the standard of love, we are sinners, we all miss the mark, and we all say so together. Lust is only one sin among many, but it is included in that confession. Our disordered behavior has compromised the church's holiness, sexual obsessions have diverted our lives from God's life, sexual blindness has left us drifting in inconsequence. The first remedy for lust is to drop the willful denial that shields our sexual lives from God, and to confess our sin to him: we have missed the mark.

When we do, we are greeted by tremendous words:

> Almighty God have mercy on you, forgive you all your sins
> through our Lord Jesus Christ, strengthen you in all good-
> ness, and by the power of the Holy Spirit keep you in eternal
> life.

For Jesus' sake, God forgives us. He forgives us, all of us, for
everything. The mark matters, and it is wholly unacceptable
that we miss it. Yet for Jesus' sake, God in fact accepts us.

A miraculous exchange occurs, when one owns one's sin to
God and hears God's response. Until then, the quality of
God's love served as a standard to identify sin as sin—love
was the mark one missed. God's response in Jesus' death and
resurrection reveals that his love is no longer against us, but
for us. Loving us, God in Christ met the mark, in our flesh.
The liturgy piles up words to make sure that everyone knows
how totally it was met:

> All glory be to thee, Almighty God, our heavenly Father, for
> that thou, of thy tender mercy, didst give thine only Son Je-
> sus Christ to suffer death upon the cross for our redemption;
> who made there, by his one oblation of himself once offered,
> a full, perfect, and sufficient sacrifice, oblation, and satisfac-
> tion, for the sins of the whole world.

The remedy for lust includes hearing that word of forgiveness deeply, as Mary heard the angel's word deep within her
body. God's forgiveness is not a legal loophole, setting justice
aside, or a sort of divine grade inflation by which everyone
gets promoted regardless. Jesus joins God's nature to ours,
and in death and resurrection turns everything upside down.

Lust pollutes the church's consecration to God. When God
forgives lust, it is by drawing us into the living gift of Christ's
own holiness. Lust sends one "looking for love in all the
wrong places," and ends in idolatry and slavery. When God
forgives lust, it is by putting his love at the center of our life.
Lust robs love of vision and purpose, leaving sex aimless.

When God forgives lust, it draws us into his great purpose: to reconcile all things to himself in Jesus Christ.

In Jesus Christ, God forgives and accepts us wholly, sinners that we are, no matter how inevitably and repeatedly we miss the mark. To receive him, all we need to do is turn to him in belief and trust. Martin Luther coined the phrase *simul iustus et peccator*, simultaneously righteous and sinner, to describe the life of faith in Christ. Lust, like any of the deadly sins, makes people miss the mark. In Christ they are forgiven, accepted as his own, delighted in as his children. That is not because the mark has been moved so that we can hit it more easily, but because the mark itself—God's eternal Law, Wisdom, Son, the Second Person of the Trinity—became one of us, died for us, rose for us. Jesus is the remedy for lust.

Knowing we are forgiven does not mean giving up the struggle against lust. Forgiveness is not a blank check for sin; it is a new relationship with the living God in which lust can have no permanent role. In Christ's indwelling, one is called to transformation. Not that any technique or exercise will make one hit the bullseye perfectly every time! Practice does not make perfect; God alone will do that, in resurrection. But God delights even in the imperfect love, the partial good that his people can do now. By grace I may improve my aim a bit—stop hitting other people with my arrows, anyway, and stop shooting myself through the foot.

In archery, aim matters. The Latin word our forbears used for aim, *intentio*, included both the direction in which one pointed the arrow and the power with which one stretched back the bowstring to impel it. The same word was used by spiritual writers to describe the direction of one's will. The mark toward which one pointed one's being, the aim toward which one's powers stretched—that was one's "intention." In handling sin, what was crucial was intention: is one aiming one's being at God, or at something else?

When God draws our intention into his own, that implies his presence in the interior place where people think and feel, yearn and fear, desire and love. Those are deep waters, over which the Holy Spirit broods, where old chaos and new creation struggle together. Intention is shaped by many forces, internal and external, which we only dimly understand and partially control. Only God can reshape lust into love like his own.

Yet there are some levels of the inner life that are a little more amenable to our own cooperative shaping than others. It helps considerably to have well-formed beliefs and standards for sexual life, born of Scripture, tradition, and reason. One can choose to live within sacramental structures—marriage or celibacy—that support the transformation. Yet neither consciously-held ideals nor approved forms for sexual life solve the mystery of lust. One's imagination often whirls around quite different values. The media blitz from outside dazzles our hearts with sexual images. Images bubble out of our unconscious; sexual ambitions and angers swirl in eddies outside the current of God's love.

Ignatius Loyola, the sixteenth-century founder of the Jesuits, thought that the direction of one's life was determined by the contents of the imagination more than by one's theoretical ideals. He worked with many Christians who were ostensibly orthodox Catholics, but whose lives were in fact ruled by their glittering internal images of sexual beauty, military prowess, economic wealth. What one cultivates in one's heart is usually what will grow.

Jonathan Edwards once said that he could not keep birds from flying over his head, but he did not have to let them build nests in his hair. We can tend to our imaginations. A gentle, tranquil renunciation can grow out of God's forgiveness: letting some thoughts go their own way, drawing others into the full current of God's love, exorcising others by invoking the power of the cross. This includes being alert and critical of the sexual messages bombarding us through the media. We can do our best to stay away from some of those images altogether, by avoiding encounters that we know will deeply mark the imagination: pornography, for example. Yet there is no way entirely to escape the barrage of sexual symbols and messages that manipulate us. That calls instead for vigilant, critical, prayerful interaction with what we see and hear, think and dream. Images that mean to misshape our character may be argued with, supplemented, and consciously held in counterpoise with God's love.

One weeds a garden, however, not to leave bare earth but so that other plants can flourish. In fact it is only when flowers are really well established, with strong roots to get the nutrients and a canopy of leaves to catch the sun, that weed seedlings slow down. Vigilance against lustful thoughts is less important than bringing into our hearts the stories and images of God's wisdom and love. Meditate on God's longing for justice, the sort of love that freed his beloved from slavery. That story is powerful. Give it room to grow, and see if it does not begin to reshape an imagination formed by dreams of sexual self-aggrandizement and manipulation.

Meditate on God's faithfulness. Many of us have no trust in covenant at all. None of the various sexual cultures that form us place much weight on faithfulness. We are the children of divorce. Some of us move from person to person, experience to experience, without making promises at all. I think such changes reinforce a pervasive despair beneath the surface of current life, an acceptance of deception, self-shrinking, and distrust. But God's love keeps promises forever, through all changes and chances. Story upon story from Israel's life is of God's covenant-keeping. In the face of rejection and judgment, God found deeper ways to keep covenant, until the deepest of all ways in Jesus. The Psalter is full of meditations on the faithfulness of God's love. In sickness, in times of terrible threat, in seasons of peace and joy, the

Psalmist turned to God, told God the truth, remembered who God was and what God had done, and found the solid rock of God's faithful love under his feet.

Meditate on God's faithfulness in love. Dwell on it, wrestle with him about it as you mediate on the stories and your experience of yourself and others. Speak the Psalms as your own, letting them give shape to your spirit. Slowly, through meditation on God's Word, brooding with God's Spirit, the solid ground of God's love will begin to emerge from the waters of lust, and a new world can be born.

Chapter 4

Avarice

Linda's bumper sticker says it all: "Born to Shop!" Six days she labors and does her work, but on the sabbath day she heads for the shopping mall. Once within the gates, Linda walks along the polished marble floors, entranced. Store after store, level upon level open up: windows shine and beckon. Rainbows of clothing, ranks upon ranks of shoes, gleaming arches of knives, silken lingerie folding in softer light, bookshops and theaters and little ethnic food counters stretch and turn out of sight. All thought of her old life outside—tough job, difficult relationships—drops away. She walks, wanting...wanting.

Once, a few years ago, Linda's mother was short of cash and made her wear a year-old dress to a big party. She had been dizzy and sick. All that night she had sat in her old clothes, empty of the beauty her friends caught from their fresh silk. Never again that hollow, dark, ugly feeling! She wants the best for herself. If she is feeling low or out of sorts, it is the mall that heals. There are no clocks there, no sun by day or moon by night, for the mall is lit by the glory of the merchandise. The marble pavement and glittering lights pull Linda on, with miles of radiant things to see, to want, to have, to be.

The third of the seven deadly sins is avarice, also known as covetousness. Like the first two, it is seated in the material level of human life. Unlike lust or gluttony, however, avarice does not feed directly on bodily hungers. It has more to do with the fact that, since we ourselves are material, we are naturally involved in the material order, and must relate to material things. We must work with them, use them, own them. We have the perilous gift of creating things, of forming dust and then breathing our own spirit into them and giving them life. Avarice is that natural human relation to material things gone wrong, the splitting of our creativity and our relation to material creation off from the Creator.

— In the Beginning —

To understand what has gone wrong between us and matter, we need to begin with what is right. "In the beginning, God created the heavens and the earth." The book of Genesis opens with two stories of creation, similar but a bit different in focus from each other. In the first story God's Word creates primeval light. Thereafter, God calls into being order upon order within the world, from dry land to plants to birds to animals. As the apex, the last act, God creates humanity, and then rests from his labor. The second story starts with humanity at the center, created first; and then, surrounding *Adam* (the Hebrew word for primal humanity), God creates all the living things that are woven with human life. The refrain echoes again and again, as each fresh step of creation occurs: "And God saw that it was good."

These stories are beautiful and mysterious, full of many meanings. They offer several perspectives on humanity's relation to material things. On the one hand, God creates us, and so we are dependent upon him for our being. His purposes for creation as a whole include us. Clearly we were meant to take joy in having been willed into existence by God, joy in receiving being from the Giver, glad to be made and to know our maker. On the other hand, we are involved with everything else created. We exist in the midst of all the orders of the world, from the first light to the animals brought forth from the ground, and we are part of them. The second story in Genesis underlines it: we humans are unambiguously material. It is "out of the dust of the ground" that God forms *Adam*.

Dust is a good word for matter. There is nothing "spiritual" about it. "Remember that dust thou art, and to dust shalt thou return." We share a common plane of existence with the things around us, bricks or sunsets, forests or septic tanks. They are real, and so are we, real in the same way. Both my foot and the shoe that covers it are the same kind of thing, as indeed is the dirt beneath them both. We are related, we are real together. According to the story that situation is of God's devising, and he calls it "good."

Yet the story does not end with a heap of dust shaped by divine fingers. God breathes the "breath of life" into what he has fashioned, and only then does *Adam* become a living being. In Hebrew, the word for "breath" and "spirit" is the same. As our breath is our life, so God's Life is his Spirit. It is the breathing of that life into material nostrils, a share in God's Spirit, that makes us truly human. We are material, but that is not all we are. True human life is related to dust, but turned toward God. Knowing God and loving him, delighting in him, gladly relating to him as creatures and as his children, is as basic a constituent to human existence as matter. As a result we have a share in God's transcendence in creation. We are conscious. We know ourselves and our world, we are alive with thought and purpose. We can recognize material existence and understand it, shape it, relate to it with vision and purpose. Neither side of human life, material or spiritual, is alien to the other. Neither can be wholly collapsed into the other. Our eyes turn both ways: to God and to the world created around us.

Human beings thus have a peculiar role in relation to material things. Since we are material, in the story God assigns us certain material things for food. But getting food calls for work: shaping matter to meet material need, and to preserve the order God intends. Adam and Eve are set in the garden to till it and keep it. Earth has to be turned, seed sown, crops harvested; normal damage is repaired, trees thinned and pruned, hedges maintained. Once outside the Garden of Eden, moreover, we are vulnerable to threats and disasters that require foresight and control. We have to work so that we can live in the material world and so that it can be kept by us as God intends.

That shaping of the world is a deeper matter than just meeting obvious needs. Our first parents tilled a garden— have you ever planted one yourself? Imagination lays out the walks, the beds for the iris, the pools; it plans the rows of vegetables in the back. Muscles turn the soil and give physical shape to it. Weeding and squirrel-chasing protect it, once laid out and planted. In the end, anonymous dirt has become a place for Eve and Adam's children to breathe, to gather food, to meet visitors while walking in the cool of the day. Not unlike God, we ourselves form dust and breathe some of our own spirit into it.

Human beings are creators within God's creation. Food and clothing and shelter do not spring up from the soil without human thought and effort, and once they are made they bear the character of their makers. No two weavers' cloth is quite the same. This is true of dresses and apple pies and brick houses. They are matter shaped for human use, and they bear the marks of the human life and spirit that created them. A dress may be graceful, a pie wholesome, a house resonant with a family's life. This is spirit in matter, in a way; breath in dust. A poet can weave sounds (themselves quite physical) into a fabric of meaning that exists as itself, irreducible. Michelangelo, they said, could make stone breathe.

When I was a teenager wandering in Europe, I saw my first painting by Rembrandt. It was of a young woman bathing. Light flooded from her white shift and from her flesh, filling the warm browns of the background. The painting was suffused with the artist's love, his sexual wonder, his worship. That painting is a material thing. It is canvas and pigment. In principle, it could be bought or stolen, owned by anybody. Yet the old paint and cloth have small intrinsic value. The only reason that anyone would want the thing is because of what Rembrandt, from within himself, made out of paint and cloth. His own self, his vision and his love, became an object. Some aspect of himself was "objectivized." When I saw the painting centuries later, I saw that part of him and answered to his call. When we create, to some extent we put ourselves into our work; it is something we recognize, seek, define. We may subsequently become strangers to the thing, "alienated" from it, but when it is first created, it is our own. We have kneaded dust and breathed our spirit into it, and it is in our image. From that depth come wonders, and also (in this world beyond Eden) monsters.

— Possession —

A curious feature of the creation stories in Genesis is that they have little to say about possession. Private ownership cannot really enter a story about primal beings, after all. Yet the silence may be significant. Most Christians reading these stories over the centuries have concluded that private ownership was no part of the order essential to creation. For some Christian thinkers, however, such as the Augustinians, property rights were an inevitable feature of greater social complexity; for others, such as the Spiritual Franciscans, property came only with sin. Scripture does not say. Yet possession is close to the center of the sin of avarice.

Westerners now take the idea of private property for granted, and the absence of it as an inconceivable tyranny. Not all Christians have agreed, however, and we do well to stand back from current arrangements and imagine our lost Eden. Could humans own things, in a world without sin? Or is possession essentially selfish, in itself the root of avarice? Would it be possible to possess things privately in a world that had never fallen away from God and did not know avarice? Our desire to possess, as things are now, is always infected with our rebellion against God. Was there ever an alternative way, a right possession that has not been corrupted by avarice?

When people create, they become deeply involved with what they make. When we plant a garden, it is not only our sweat that goes into it, but our mind and skill as well. "You really put yourself into it!" we say. We give distinctive shape to the things we create, and so it is natural that we should consider them ours.

All the more, things are "mine" when they have become involved in my history, my own personal experience. A thief recently stole a pendant watch that my wife had been given by her grandmother. The insurance company faithfully sent us a check, so that we could buy a replacement. Yet of course nothing, not even an identical copy, could replace the old one. By long use it had become the sign of the women who had worn it and whose lives were connected with it—who in that deeper sense had "owned" it. Thus it belonged properly to my wife, who had loved those women. By stripping the watch from those relationships, out of its proper ownership, the thief made it anonymous, less real, less fully created.

Creation and thus ownership is always communal and social as well as individual. Needs are shared, labor is shared, control and administration are shared. Even the most idiosyncratic of painters with the most iconoclastic vision depends on someone else to weave canvas, and a culture to provide a visual language for him or her to shatter. My wife's watch had been made by many hands, and it was her relationship with her grandmother that made it so dear to her. There is no truly "private" property, even outside of Eden. One does not worship the works of one's hands, but one shares them with others, as God does. Yet within this framework, it is natural enough for us to have an attachment to things as being in some sense our own.

It is at this point that avarice attacks. Avarice is idolatry—putting something created in God's place. At its deepest, it uses material things as idols, or as a disguised form of self-worship. Avarice treats something that is not God as if it were. That displaces God, and turns the whole story of creation on its head. Throughout the Old Testament runs a vein of astonishment that human beings try to worship created things as God. Israel had contempt for nations that, like Egypt, worshiped cats and crocodiles, or the local pagans who worshiped the forces of nature like lightning or sex. Only God was Lord, not the things God created. But pagans even worshiped things that their own hands had made, literal "idols" that had been carved out of wood or cast out of metal. A man cuts down a tree, makes part into a footstool, makes another part into a statue to worship. Incredible! Yet Israel, too, found the impulse strong. The second commandment, which prohibited carved or cast images of any created thing for worship, was no sooner given at Sinai than Israel was making and worshiping the golden calf at the foot of the mountain. People worship what they own.

— You Can't Take It With You —

Brian is a stockbroker. Since his early twenties, his chief goal has been to attain complete financial independence by the time he is forty. This is not a search for security—Brian wants wealth as an achievement in itself. A personal net worth in the millions will make him a man of substance, a man of recognized standing and achievement. To that end he is disciplined: tough but discreet, careful about his dealings with inside tips or with the IRS, meticulous in research and preparation, quick and ruthless in execution. As a result he has made a great deal of money for other people, and is on the verge of making at least as much for himself. He loves the thought of the money, growing, potent, to be handled like a spirited horse. It would not be fair to say that money is his whole life. He can take vacations at times. He enjoys his children when he sees them. His divorce was a major setback because of the division of assets that followed, but nothing distracts him for long from his passion. He does not often think of death, but he means his estate to be his memorial.

Brian is an idolater. His values are determined by his god. Even his relative honesty is designed solely to avoid jeopardizing his financial situation. His human relationships are shaped by the drive for money, not vice versa. That worship fills him and shapes him. In Brian's tacit eschatology, the heavenly future is when his money is measureless, omnipotent, eternal. Money determines what he is and what he wants to be—it casts him in its image and likeness.

Augustine thought that human beings treat created things as substitutes for God. We prefer an immediate, visible glory we can grasp for ourselves to the invisible glory of God. Things carry something of their maker with them, whether the maker is God or a human being. That "something" can be grasped for its own sake, apart from the maker; when it displaces God, it is idolatry. A woman who catches a reflected glimpse of God's beauty through a certain view of redwoods down a certain river may ignore God, take those trees as the beauty she seeks, and spend her life buying the property. This applies to human products as well; once we put our wisdom and spirit into them, it is possible to put them in God's place.

It may be, however, that we also adore what we feel we lack in ourselves and seek elsewhere; when we own things, we hope to share in the life they carry or convey. When I was a lumpish teenager, above all things I wanted a Mercedes-Benz: fast, crisp, powerful, designed with precision and grace. If I could drive it as my own, that grace would be mine. In the same way, when one pulls on a pair of immaculate white linen trousers, fresh and crisp, one shares their purity—without needing to acquire a pure heart.

Idolatry is not an innocent mistake, Augustine saw. Human beings often prefer idols because they are things they themselves can own and dominate—Victorian houses, powerful cars, toys, stock futures—as one cannot own or dominate God. When we take these for our idols, the self is left in control. One may bow down to them and worship them, but one never really forgets that they were made and bought, and who is still in charge.

The sages who wrote the Old Testament books of Proverbs, Wisdom, and Ecclesiasticus had originally accepted at face value the sensible theory that those who did right would receive God's blessing, including the blessing of material prosperity. Later they came to reconsider that idea. The problem was obvious: some good people died poor and some wicked people lived high on the hog all their days. The sages began to look to the last things, death and an eschatological future in which a sovereign God would redress the balance:

> Do not be afraid when some become rich,
> > when the wealth of their houses increases.
> For when they die they will carry nothing away;
> > their wealth will not go down after them.
> Though in their lifetime they count themselves happy—
> > for you are praised when you do well for yourself—

> they will go to the company of their ancestors,
>   who will never again see the light.
> Mortals cannot abide in pomp;
>   they are like the animals that perish. (Ps. 49:16-20)

Furthermore, the sages began to notice the effects of wealth on the wealthy. It seemed to bring arrogance, callousness, and self-glorification. Far from heightening a sense of thankful dependence on God, it did the reverse. Accumulation of goods brings power, reputation, and glory—an apparent share in the goodness and potency of the things possessed. Yet one's possessions fall from one's grasp at death when the spirit returns to God its maker, when the dead go down to Sheol.

Many of Jesus' stories picked up this tradition, and Luke in particular remembered what he said. To the rich man, who built extra barns to contain his grain and goods and who said to himself, "Soul, you have ample goods laid up for many years; relax, eat, drink, be merry," God's answer was blunt. "Fool! This very night your life is being demanded of you. And the things you have prepared, whose will they be?" Death exposes avarice pitilessly. The story illustrated Jesus' word: "Take care! Be on your guard against all kinds of greed; for one's life does not consist in the abundance of possessions" (Luke 12:15-20).

Jesus' own life, the life he required of his disciples, was one of renunciation of the whole cycle of accumulation and possession of material goods as the basis of the life of this world. He never condemned material things themselves, and he never condemned ownership as such. But his explicit words and the deliberate shape of his life condemned avarice. Jesus' own homelessness contrasted plainly with those who built great houses on the sand of this world. His act of guerilla theater at the Temple, overturning the money-changers' tables, damned the divisive and exclusive power of money. It also exposed the sanctified greed of religion as a collaboration with the present age. His words were as clear as his actions: "Sell all that you have, and give to the poor, and come, follow me."

People's resistance to this message revealed their paradoxical rebellion and slavery. It exposed avarice's deepest root: the refusal to be dependent on God. It made clear what God's view of it is: rejection of his kingdom.

Ownership did not interest Jesus. What did interest him was God, and the world that his Father created. From Jesus there shines out the same truths that fill the Genesis stories of creation. There is only one who is God. He is the absolute center of human life, as of all things. He is Lord, without rivals. His majesty and power do not admit of comparison. At the same time he is as close to the world as can be, as intimate and involved in the life of his creatures as parents are in their children's. The rest of creation is still glad to depend on God's care. We alone have decided to worry about ourselves:

> Therefore I tell you, do not be anxious about your life, what you shall eat, nor about your body, what you shall put on. For life is more than food, and the body more than clothing. Consider the ravens; they neither sow nor reap, they have neither storehouse nor barn, and yet God feeds them. Of how much more value are you than the birds!...Consider the lilies, how they grow; they neither toil nor spin; yet I tell you, even Solomon in all his glory was not arrayed like one of these. (Luke 12:22-24, 27)

The anxiety about providing for our needs, the laborious effort to construct our own glory, are a miserable contrast with a life received gladly from God and lived simply toward him.

Jesus showed compassion toward those who were hungry and in need, often by meeting their own concrete, material needs. Yet he also showed compassion toward their anxiety, their consuming preoccupation with possessions. What he chiefly tried to teach them was faith. The ground of their anxiety was refusal to trust God and depend on him. For Jesus, in contrast, a life of renunciation, of deliberate, trusting, believing poverty, simply was to depend on his Father in complete freedom, fully open to God's future.

Jesus' final material renunciation was his physical death. His resurrection in the flesh was the first fruits of God's healing of our relationship to matter. In Jesus, the dust of the ground has the breath of eternal life. What has gone wrong in avarice, in him is set right.

Yet Christians have not given very much thought to the place of material possessions in the new creation. Liberation theologians have been giving a great deal of attention to God's kingdom in this world, in which systemic avarice must be destroyed for the sake of its victims. But for them, as for the rest of the theological tradition, there are few visions of a transformed future for material things—of the human power of creation, here corrupted by avarice, there healed and transfigured. What has dawned, in a few writers, is the hope that in his kingdom God would resurrect a material order in which avarice could not grow. Some early Christians (as well as some modern ones!) thought of the new order as one of incredible, unlimited material prosperity. God's overwhelming material generosity would make our own almost inevitable— very good news for the wretched of the earth. Others, like Gregory of Nyssa, have thought that the whole basis of material existence would be transformed, that matter itself would be recreated and glorified. Still others have taken up the hints in the New Testament that our priesthood in creation would be restored, and that it would grow to include the whole cosmos.

Yet surely the chief difference will be the immediate presence of God's glory. If we see God clearly, all the derivative glories of creation will give witness to the One in a way not admitting of idolatry. The book of Revelation shows the vast avarice of Babylon destroyed utterly, and the New Jerusalem a pure glory that welcomes all other true glories within it. "By its light shall the nations walk; and the kings of the earth shall bring their glory into it, and its gates shall never be shut" (Rev. 21:24-25). What human beings make, what human spirit breathes into matter, will be welcome there. For there it can do no harm, pose no danger of idolatry and avarice. God is so utterly at the city's heart, so wholly the center of its citizens' being, that no false alternative could occur. "The city has no need of sun or moon to shine upon it, for the glory of God is its light, and its lamp is the Lamb" (Rev. 21:23).

─── Remedies ───

We do not yet live in the New Jerusalem. Many of us are Christians who intermittently want to take our baptism seriously, but our work, recreation, entertainment, and hopes for the future are so tied up in the cycle of getting and spending that an existence free of avarice is beyond our imagination. Our material needs may be desperate and immediate, as among the millions of Christians in Ethiopia, or they may simply be all-absorbing anxieties, as they are for millions of Christians in Europe and North America. Yet we mean to have faith in Jesus Christ. We want to be in solidarity with the new creation, which has no place for greed. Recognizing our unbelief and avarice, fostered and magnified enormously by our culture, what can we do now?

The first thing we can do is to accept God's act of liberation in Jesus Christ, and to trust him to save us from a trap from which we cannot save ourselves. We are caught in a system we cannot overturn simply by an act of the will, with guilt toward each other and toward God for our solidarity with the oppression in which we inevitably live. I know as well as one can by reading what exploitation of black gold miners in South Africa is like; I cannot remove the South African gold from my wedding ring. I know well how migrant fruit pickers have to work and for how little, because I have done it, but rinsing my lettuce and tomatoes will not remove their sweat. We can, however, believe that for Jesus' sake God counts us as forgiven and beloved, now.

What must flow from that faith, though, is freedom, and not only freedom from guilt. Our freedom includes genuine trust in God, which implies an end to idolatry. "In God we trust" is mockery when printed on a dollar bill, given the attitudes of most of us to money. Sometimes God presents a chance for freedom by permitting a major change in our material fortunes. Nothing poses the issue of avarice more clearly than losing a job, or getting one. Then comes the choice: whom do you trust? Who is your god?

Deprivation is evil, but God may use it to pose good questions. It is painful to have to walk over broken idols, but pain may be a useful warning. Empty hands—even those unwillingly empty—can reach out to God, and find out that God was already reaching for us. One has a choice: to trust God, or to scrabble more bitterly after the old gods. Much the same can be true of increasing prosperity, though it is perhaps more dangerous. If one comes into money, it can stimulate thanksgiving and open generosity of heart, should one choose to depend on God instead of idolizing one's wealth and oneself.

Responding in faith to loss and gain is one thing; deliberate framing of a style of life is another. In Christ, we are free to choose new ways of living toward material possessions. For this the church holds out two choices: two traditions, deliberately chosen, that have existed side by side from the beginning. One is the radical way of voluntary poverty, and the other the way of stewardship. Either can be deliberately cultivated as a way of living in hope toward the new creation while still resident in the old order. Both mean to put a stop to the effects of avarice now; both take God's side against the demonic power still at work in the world.

Poverty, the radical response, witnesses to the sheer reality of God's kingdom and lives in immediate, visible dependence on God's grace. "Sell what you have, and give to the poor, and come, follow me." Many thousands of Christians in all ages have literally done just that. Most of the apostles did, following Jesus' own example, and so did some of the Jerusalem community and groups of widows. In the fourth century, the deserts began to fill with men and women who found getting and spending a demonic slavery unworthy of the sons and daughters of God. Roman ladies of the senatorial class and Saxon knights, runaway centurions and small farmers turned their backs on possessions and entered monasteries, never to own anything again. Francis of Assisi loved Lady Poverty just as he loved her Lord, and found in absolute possessionlessness the freedom that nothing in the world could give him.

The Christian church urgently needs some of its members to be *visibly* poor in an act of free renunciation. We need visible examples of dependence on God alone, people who trust themselves to God's care without compromise, as Jesus did. In this world, in which the value of persons is defined in economic terms alone, we need people who witness that only God defines human value. Nothing will make that case more clearly than the freedom of Christian poverty. We need people who will show that the world is the Lord's by themselves owning none of it. This does not always have to be in the form of lifelong and absolute renunciation of all possessions. Christians may leave their things for a space to win freedom by the Spirit and to serve. Young farmers in Russia once came far south to the monasteries of Mt. Athos for a few months or years to learn detachment and prayer. The Peace Corps, short term missions, and urban community work all offer the possibility to turn toward the New Creation, where people worship God and not the things that their hands have made, and are thus free to serve others in generosity of spirit. Yet there is a particular value in having some Christians in our midst whose baptism has expressed itself in an unconditional turn toward God's future and the consequent renunciation of the orders of this present age in life-long, vowed poverty.

Stewardship is the other traditional way of living with material possessions. Stewards rule and care for something on behalf of its true owner. Christian stewardship is to live out Adam and Eve's lost vocation by ruling and caring for a share of God's world. We urgently need Christians who deliberately choose to live in the midst of this world as if God really were the Lord and creator of it all. We are not the owners and makers of all things; God is. What one has, one holds in trust from him and on behalf of others. Our creativity is to mirror his, our generosity his own.

Stewards will use creation in a way that displays its transparency to the glory of God. One way is by praise: constant thanks for pure water, clean earth, well-designed buildings, birds wading in wet marshes, anything lovingly and skillfully made. Stewards praise and thank God; they praise and thank God's other creatures, human beings, whose care and creativity shares in God's glory. Closely related to this way is the way of justice. Stewards can reflect God's glory by working to open creation and creative work to all of God's children. Gardens are good things, but better when others can enjoy them, and best when others can get land to plant their own.

Either call—poverty or stewardship—implies genuine asceticism. There is no way in which we can be exposed to the barrage of the media and not find our hungers expanding irrationally. Shopping malls may cultivate avarice as brothels do lust. If, dispirited, we begin to seek stability by buying good wool clothing, or intellectual power by buying a computer, or athleticism by buying shoes, it is time to catch our breath alone with God. An hour of real talk with a friend, without looking at her clothes or car, spent reading her face and not her jewelry, can help, too. If pursuit of unnecessary wealth takes you away from prayer, from service, from true enjoyment of God and his creation, from honest work, then it is time to act. Find that friend, and talk over the direction of your energy and loyalty and what really deserves them. Then make one specific change in your schedule, as a concrete step in the redirection of the worship of your life.

One very small beginning in the war against avarice is within the reach of almost everyone: the tithe. The principle behind it has been clear from the beginning of Israel's life. Everything that God's people acquire comes from God. The tithe means to return one tenth of those acquisitions to God, as an offering owed in duty and thanksgiving. When I offer God ten percent of all that I receive, it reminds me in a concrete, pungent way that God is the maker and lord of all that I have. I depend on God concretely, and I give him thanks concretely. It also acts out my duty to share with others. It helps to form a spirit of generosity, not the least important sign of growing faith.

At the Eucharist we put tithes into the plate and the canned goods in the basket, and they are taken forward to the altar to be offered to God with the bread and wine. That is a rich symbol of the offering of the whole material and human world to God in Christ. It is a concrete gift to God's work and an appeal for God's forgiveness for the avarice infecting our world. Still more, it is a sign of our common priesthood, symbolizing the priestly offering that I intend my creative work in the world to be, offering the things of this world to God. It points to the day when all creation will once again be restored to its integrity, gladly offering itself to the God who makes it and blesses it and calls it good.

Avarice means to turn creation into a sort of black hole, sucking everything into itself. Jesus' death and resurrection have turned that hole inside out. His risen body breaks all the old limitations and addictions of fallen materiality. God's infinite generosity through him is preparing a new creation, a new heaven and a new earth in which humans will be truly at home, in which idolatry, waste, greed, and misery will never enter again. Christians are called to live in hope, and thus to be free from avarice.

--- Chapter 5 ---

Anger

Anger is popular. The generation now reaching retirement age was taught to restrain its anger, even to deny it altogether. Anger was bad, hurtful, destructive; one was not to feel that way, and certainly not to express it if one did. Since the sixties, however, there has been a strong reaction. Virtually every self-help manual urges people to discover their buried anger and get it out, while political movements are rediscovering anger as a source of power. Tell your husband what you really feel about his insensitivity; sound off at the staff meeting about the way management treats employees; flip the bird at bad drivers in heavy traffic. Anger is in.

One exception to the new stylishness of rage is the church's theology, where a god of wrath is still not popular. Not that this is new; Christian theologians have always been embarrassed about the Bible's portrayal of an angry God. Gregory of Nyssa in the East and Augustine of Hippo in the West tried to reduce God's wrath to a fault in human perception. God was free of any such passion; it was only that sinful people experienced God as angry. Since the Wars of Religion of the seventeenth century, there has been a major political incentive to deny God's wrath and create instead a god who will stop religious wars and bless the prosperous peace of bourgeois Europe. The rebellion of Neo-Orthodox theologians like Barth or Niebuhr against the god of sweetness and light had no real effect on this tendency in the mainline churches. Sermons, hymns, and liturgies have been carefully edited to remove anger. In the Episcopal Church, which for a long time stuck doggedly to the regular reading of the whole Psalter in the Daily Office, the angriest verses of the Psalms are now marked for omission. Anger is becoming healthy and powerful and even stylish outside of church, but no one wants an angry God.

The result is confusion, because Christians do not know whether their anger is good or evil. They are told that they are made in God's image, and at the same time to own their anger. Then they are told that there is no anger in the One whose nature they ought to reflect. They are called to be the children of a peace-loving God; yet to be psychologically healthy and politically active, they must themselves be angry.

Anger that is right serves and protects something good. As long as the cosmos throws up rebellion against God's goodness, there will be a need for right wrath. There is also an anger that is wrong, an anger that flowers into one of the seven deadly sins. Sinful anger sides with the rebellion.

---- Right Wrath ----

Aristotle observed that animals are "irritable." That is, if you poke an animal, it will respond. It naturally protects itself against threat. Any child soon learns the truth of the ancient bit of wisdom, "Let sleeping dogs lie." If one hits a dog, if one pulls it away from its food dish, if one hurts its puppies, the dog may bite. It defends what it needs to live, an "irritable" response that extends beyond itself to its young. Indeed, if the dog learns to love the child, then anyone who threatens the child may feel its teeth. The angry response is natural, nature being as it is. Indeed it is essential, if animals are to survive.

Human beings are animals, and so they are "irritable." They act to protect their integrity. If their being or essential activities are threatened, they respond in anger. If someone comes at another with a knife or steals her food or harms her child, she will act in an angry way: knock the knife aside, grab the food back, defend the child. Social life is a vast effort to make this angry response unnecessary, and to channel it helpfully when it occurs. I can sit in a restaurant munching my hamburger in peace, not fearing that the man sitting next to me will wrest it from my grasp; he has been taught not to behave that way. He knows that he has no "right" to take my hamburger, and that he will get into trouble if he does. I do not need to be angry. Yet society holds a corporate anger in reserve for those who violate the conventions. If the man *does* grab my hamburger, the police may come.

In a sense, the love of social justice is this same anger transposed to a higher level. Everyone's integrity and essential needs are to be guarded, not just one's own. Social anger does not only protect one's self, or even blood kin, but the integrity of one's neighbor. It is right to defend a neighbor who is being mugged or a community that is being denied jobs or housing. Fury may be strong for the right. Rage gives energy to ward away evil and to respond to injustice. This may seem a dangerous claim, when one sees automatic weapons turned on schoolyards, or has to live in a social system poisoned by hatred, like Lebanon or Washington, D.C. Anger's energy, like nuclear fission, may seem to take on a power of its own and destroy the very things it ought to serve. Yet in a social world, there could be no justice without right anger. Right anger is commitment to human integrity and the social fabric, not the reverse. It acts to defend life and justice. In this sense, it is possible to be angry in love. Thus angry feelings are not necessarily sinful. Neither are the actions born of such anger. The kingdom of God has not yet come, and until it does, anger is the right response to some realities.

The Bible is bursting with examples of right wrath. Abraham used violence to rescue Lot from rival warlords. The Torah did not suppress anger; it channelled anger a thousand ways, from "an eye for an eye" to the blood sacrifice bringing reconciliation. Deborah routed Israel's oppressors in the days of the judges; the prophet Amos furiously damned the wealthy exploiters of the poor within Israel. John the Baptist used vitriolic language against self-serving religious leaders—as did Jesus, who wept with anger at unbelief. Peter cursed Ananias and Sapphira for their hypocrisy; Paul hoped that those who forced Gentiles to be circumcised would slip with the knife and maim themselves. In the Bible's human detail, anger is powerful: terribly volatile, but strong to assert the right of good against evil. It all depends on how that force stands in relationship to God.

The God of the whole Bible is a God of wrath. The old truism that the angry God of the Old Testament was replaced by Jesus' God of love is an anti-semitic fiction first propagated by the second-century heretic, Marcion. The Old Testament is not so lightly disentangled from the New; love is not so easily separated from anger. God does not permit his integrity of being—the unbounded reality and wisdom and love he is—to be perverted by lies about him. God's love for Israel brought his judgment and wrath on the Egyptians who enslaved them. According to Hosea, God furiously broke his marriage to Israel with a decree of divorce when Israel flouted his love. God's love for the world brought the judgment and death of his Son. Right wrath grows from commitment to the good; it is born of God's wisdom and love. There can be no theology of liberation, no God who sides with the poor and oppressed, without an angry God.

God repels all assaults on his purposes, his love: the great themes and stories of the Bible are simply incomprehensible without a God who acts. Paul merely brings the whole biblical tradition to a point when, in Romans, he begins his exposition of the Gospel with a powerful essay on God's anger:

> For the wrath of God is revealed from heaven against all ungodliness and wickedness of those who by their wickedness suppress the truth. (Rom. 1:18)

The wrath of God is positive and active, destroying the lies and wrongs generated by human beings who reject God. From the third chapter of Genesis to the last words of the Apocalypse, the Bible is woven through with God's right wrath, judging and punishing the sin that assaults his being, character, and loving purpose. When his creatures deny the central truth of reality, what the Bible calls the "glory" of God, it is like spitting against the wind. God is life and love; those who serve death and hatred can expect what Paul calls "the wrath to come."

This has odd consequences for the evaluation of human anger. On the one hand, if people are made in God's image, surely it cannot be entirely wrong to act as he does: to respond in anger to attacks on God's being and purposes and, in close relation, to attacks on the integrity and life of those made in God's image. On the other hand, Paul makes it clear in Romans 2 that everyone is party to the rebellion against God. Self-righteous people who think that they are defenders of God against the pagans are subject to God's judgment too; they are simply hypocrites instead of avowed rebels. Because of the strange texture of divinity and sin that makes up human life, human anger is always ambiguous.

Perhaps the clearest case of humans wielding right wrath is in the prophetic tradition, where prophets are called to serve as messengers of God's anger. In Amos' day, God's anger was for the social elite. Dishonest weights and measures, tolerance of gang crime, legalized fraud in real estate, and the relentless pursuit of pleasure all came down to one thing: contempt for God, his covenant, and his poor. God's response was unambiguous: sheer fury. Amos was sent to tell Israel that God was going to destroy them. In doing so, Amos' fury was God's own, and it was right. In the nineteenth century, abolitionists like the Grimké sisters and Frederick Douglass brought a similar word to slave-owning America. God was about to "trample out the vintage where the grapes of wrath are stored," a wine of human blood. Their anger was right.

Consider Jesus' anger. There was no question of him "losing his temper"; the wave of fury that overwhelms people and their right purposes is not reflected in the gospels' stories about him. It was the disciples who tried to get him to call down fire from heaven on a recalcitrant village; he would not consider it. The anger Jesus did express depended exclusively on God. He refused to start a violent revolution, and went to his death without calling on the violence of men or of angels. He did not defend his own integrity and purposes; apart from God, he did not have any. Yet there is no reason at all to think that Jesus was not angry, or that the rebellious powers that dominated the world were not about to be overthrown, and rightly. Yet it was God who would do the overthrowing. To Pontius Pilate and the Sanhedrin at his trial, Jesus' refusal to compromise his person or mission was, in a deep sense, angry. That utterly unmoved, silent, irrefragable presence was the rock on which the present order would break: it was the terrible silence of God's wrath.

The mysterious and difficult fact that God acts in anger to assert his being, truth, and purpose makes it clear that not all human anger is wholly wrong. But it can easily go wrong. In the eleventh century, Peter the Hermit raised up thousands of peasants against "God's enemies" in the Holy Land. The smoking ruins of Jewish communities down the Rhine and the eventual massacre of the peasants by Saracens—who also believed that God willed it—should not encourage other crusaders. Thomas Cranmer signed the death warrant of "heretics" for teaching a eucharistic theology virtually identical to the one Queen Mary later killed him for believing. The sinner's self-determining mind can turn God's word into self-serving ideology. The denouncer of passions is himself enslaved by passion. Even among the oppressed, the cry for vindication is mixed with envy and mutual exploitation. Right wrath is hard to find.

Feelings of anger, like any other strong feelings, may be right in origin and yet go wrong easily. They are exceedingly difficult to manage in Christ's way; the pull of selfishness is too strong. One's sense of justice is keenest in one's own cause. In Bosnia people fight to defend their families, their neighborhoods and villages, their religions, their ancient grievances. They see what they want to see, remember only what reinforces their claims. Such blindness happens daily, on church boards, on zoning commissions, in families, among the nations of the earth. For a Christian to use wrath rightly calls for constant vigilance, the most demanding discipline of mind and will, the greatest care for communal life turned to God—and for constant prayer for forgiveness for constant failure.

— The Sin of Anger —

Lust, gluttony, and avarice all take their origin in the physical, material level of created life. The deadly sin of anger is seated in an even more significant level, and so it is more virulent. God created humans to need "helpmeets"—to live with and to depend on other human beings. The existence of others may create the potential for conflict, but before that it carries the greater blessing of companionship. Human life is necessarily social. Becoming human depends on other humans, not only for reproduction, food, and goods, but also for shared wisdom and understanding, for growth in feeling and relationship, for fun and work. To be human is to have neighbors. Anger is a sin against the gift of social life; anger has no neighbors, only enemies and obstacles.

Sinful anger is a destructive movement against a neighbor on one's own account, apart from God. It may be internal: a violent thought, consented to and enjoyed, or a settled disposition of hatred. Sinful anger may be external: murder or backbiting are both sins of anger. It may be individual, as when I enjoy the destruction of the reputation of a bishop whom I dislike, or it may be communal, as in Northern Ireland. Anger sins against the social order, in which neighbor ought to defend neighbor, and it sins against God, who is the only source of right.

Angry feelings may or may not be present in sinful anger. The Spanish have a proverb that vengeance is a dish best eaten cold. What is at issue in the deadly sin of anger are not feelings, but the intention to destroy. The sin of anger takes root in such intentions. Anger can become a permanent part of the character of a person or a nation, a disposition always ready to move into action. A woman's sense of grievance against her family may grow ever deeper, every word searched for a fresh slight, old wounds constantly reopened. She is sinfully angry as a disposition of her character. In this sense, racist whites are always "angry," maintaining a system that puts down blacks; racist blacks are always prepared to hate and blame whites who perpetuate the system. Anger becomes part of what it means to be white or black.

In sinful anger, the "irritable" response turns around a basically selfish set of assumptions about reality. The standard is set by our own determination of what is normal and right. Our own sense of self, the circumstances we consider important for maintaining that integrity, our autonomy of action, are going to be maintained no matter what. Deciding what is right is not left to God or to anyone else. Anger is also sin against God, and not only against neighbor, when it makes the self the absolute center and displaces God.

One basic expression of the deadly sin of anger is the effort to eliminate obstacles to one's self-definition and self-seeking. In this case anyone who obstructs one's goals becomes simply a barrier to be removed. This can be trivial, such as pounding on the steering wheel and cursing when some fool is blocking my exit lane in traffic. It can also be profound and ice-cold. National Socialist theologians and historians thought that the integrity of the Jewish people stood between Aryans and their cultural self-realization; they wrote history and criticism that deliberately distorted and shrank the thought and cultural role of European Jews to nothing but parasitism.

To edit a people out of history is a thoroughgoing act of anger, another kind of holocaust. A drug dealer who wants to expand his turf and so murders a competitor; a businessman who ditches an uncouth wife when she impedes his career; a sheep rancher who poisons another's animals so that his flocks can use the wells unobstructed; a professor who savages a colleague's book to enhance her own standing in the field; a country that goes to war to take a warm-water port: all of these acts of anger have a good deal in common. The self-defined self and its goals are the absolute; the neighbor is diminished, merely an obstacle to be removed. God, who created human beings to live together in mutual joy and peace, is himself just an obstruction.

Another form of anger is the attack on threats to one's self-security. Rather than trusting God or one's fellows, one strikes in order to stay safe. A pastor of my acquaintance was called to serve in a church. Immediately he dissolved all the committees and church organizations that he himself could not control. It was not that any of those organizations were particularly wrong-headed, merely that they were not headed by him. His priesthood was secure only if he had no potential rivals. That was an act of anger. When a bureaucrat sandbags a reform measure that might shrink the importance of her department, the same sort of self-protective anger is at work.

This particular form of the sin of anger has a subtle outcome in the case of racism. One of the mysteries of prejudice is why a dominant group that has harmed and even enslaved another should so adamantly continue to denigrate and harm its victims. Part of the mystery is that human beings hate those whom they have wronged. The guilt for the wrong has got to be suppressed; otherwise, it would threaten the wrongdoers' identity and status. To continue to do evil to those one has injured, to think evil of them and hate them, is a peculiar sort of self-security. It pushes away guilt, it justifies the wrong by making the victims deserve it, and it defers repentance indefinitely. Hate those you wrong: it means you won't have to change.

Another expression of sinful anger is vengeance. The proverb "Don't get mad, get even" puts it clearly. Injury or insult to my person or my people has to be repaid with interest. This sort of anger does not eliminate obstacles or defend against threats. It retaliates. If it perceives that it has suffered any sort of harm, it evens the score.

Anger at illegitimate attack and injustice is justified, but only God claims the right of vengeance. Individuals cannot act fairly when they constitute themselves as judge, jury, and executioner in their own cause. It is essential to refer the wrong to others, and above all to God, on whom right depends.

The case of corporate, institutionalized vengeance, in which human courts of law judge and punish guilt, is perhaps more ambiguous. If humans have the right to judge and punish wrong, it is only because God gives them that right. The ground of the moral order is not simply the social self-projection of a people, as if one could create one's own moral right, and then enforce it in perfect autonomy. Even the Deists who wrote the Constitution of the United States recognized that the right underlying a people's decision to judge and punish wrong is God's, a responsibility given by God to people made in his image. People cannot claim vengeance in their own name.

While the biblical tradition consistently upholds the divine basis of human judgment and punishment of wrong, it is also shot through with a clear understanding of how far wrong such legitimized vengeance can go. Tales of personal revenge and its terrible consequences abound. Yet not only private vengeance was problematic. The great Succession Narrative that stretches between 1 Samuel and 1 Kings is a fabric of revenge woven around the throne of Israel, David's deeds of blood boiling back through his own house. Murder, conspiracy, abuse of public power, the long-meditated settling of old private scores swirl around David's throne. There is no simple right in humanly administered justice, even when God's Anointed sits as judge. David was a sinner, still moved by the old rebellion, even though God had made him king of Israel.

That ambiguity of human justice's divine legitimacy and yet its blind, proud, selfish partnership in sin emerges in John's account of Jesus' trial:

> Pilate...entered his headquarters again and asked Jesus, "Where are you from?" But Jesus gave him no answer. Pilate therefore said to him, "Do you refuse to speak to me? Do you not know that I have power to release you, and power to crucify you?" Jesus answered him, "You would have no power over me unless it had been given you from above; therefore the one who handed me over to you is guilty of a greater sin." (John 19:9-11)

Pilate's right to avenge wrong did come from God. But since his own political cowardice and ambition made him refuse God and pervert justice, a strange inversion took place. It was Jesus, the accused criminal, who pronounced the verdict—against his human judge. At that moment, God judged self-serving human "justice."

The deadly sin of anger has its overt expression in actions: in murder, in verbal assault, in job discrimination. Anger can also become a disposition. It can penetrate the bones of a resentful person; it can come to dominate their character. One of the worst effects of doing wrong to someone is that they may find their responding anger impossible to let go. Individuals or whole peoples can gnaw on old grievances, remembering them again and again, renewing them obsessively until the shape of memory and desire is permanently warped along the lines of anger. Life itself is shaped by anger; one's self is defined by anger. Few things are as terrible as knowing an old man or woman whose personality would collapse if it were not held rigid by resentment.

The final expression of sinful anger is against God. This does not necessarily mean that all angry feelings toward God are deadly, because God can work with angry feelings that are freely made known to him as the backwash of a positive relationship. Job was angry at God, but he did not turn away from God; he wanted to meet him. Sinful anger toward God wants no meeting.

— Atonement —

Sinful anger is the weapon of the false self seeking its own goals by destroying its neighbors. God's anger is not like that. His wrath is a response to human lies about him; its main purpose is to establish the truth, and thus the ground for new life.

The truth revealed through God's wrath is that God is love. God does not simply assert his integrity in anger, defending himself by destroying the liars. The deeper truth about him is that he gives and shares himself in order to turn liars to the truth. He reveals his straightness not by breaking what is crooked, but by making it straight too. God defends his integrity through the costly gift of new integrity to anyone who will find it in Jesus. God's anger achieves its end—it establishes the truth about him—in love.

Jesus' blood-sacrifice of himself reversed the curse of anger. It expressed God's eternal, accurate judgment on sin, but beneath that, the still deeper truth that God was reconciling the world to himself. God's wrath at sin's rejection of relationship with him is the storm-front of his love; God's anger is born from his commitment to the relationship that human sin denies.

> While we were still weak, at the right time Christ died for the ungodly. Indeed, rarely will anyone die for a righteous person—though perhaps for a good person someone might actually dare to die. *But God proves his love for us in that while we were sinners Christ died for us.* Much more surely then, now that we have been justified by his blood, will we be saved through him from the wrath of God. (Rom. 5:6-9)

God's right wrath asserts his integrity; but God's integrity is love.

This is the true remedy, and the only one, for the spiral of anger that twists through the world. In Palestine, in Brooklyn neighborhoods, between husband and wife, selfish anger destroys life. One person or people asserts its own integrity without God, and sparks a responding hatred. That one's own being should be grounded in God's love, and thus even anger be an expression of love, of commitment to God's purpose of reconciliation: that does not cross many minds caught up in the spiral. But admitting the justice of God's anger and making one's way to the cross opens up an entirely new possibility.

— Remedies —

Part of living toward freedom from the sin of anger is to sit more lightly to one's own present. That does not necessarily mean that Christians are always to be counseled to swallow their wrongs and wait for a distant vindication. Christians can speak and act in right wrath to assert God's truth and justice. Yet our dreams and goals, our whole view of reality, are partial and temporary by God's standards. God's anger and God's love move people beyond the self-integrity and self-needs that human anger defends to his own gift of true self and fulfillment of deepest needs in the resurrection.

One has the right to resist any attack on the integrity of being that God gives. Women who have been told that they are worthless and powerless may stand up in Christ and say, by God's making and God's reconciling I am something of value. Peoples who have been enslaved may stand up in Christ and say, God has freed us, and we ought not to be the slaves of others. To resist wrong in that way is to reject a lie contrary to God's kingdom, like Christ's own refusal to compromise the identity and mission his Father gave him. As long as people depend on God for their being and live toward a future identity and life that are in God's hands and not simply of their own making, they are right to reject evil in right wrath. Yet it is fearfully easy to cry out for "justice" while really only protecting selfishness.

How does one express right anger positively, in a way genuinely turned toward God's kingdom? Christian tradition has a divided pattern of response. The radical response is *pacifist*. It shares Jesus' witness that God alone is judge and king, and it follows his example of renouncing coercive violence. For radical Christians, it is God's kingdom alone that will heal the wounds of human violence; for us to use violence now will only leave more wounds. The only way out of the spiral of anger between nations and peoples is to renounce it altogether. If the wicked attack, radical Christians accept death; God can raise the dead. From the desert fathers and mothers to the Mennonites, and very widely indeed in the early church, the radical witness is consistent: God will defend his own people as he will. It is simply their duty to condemn wrong in right wrath, to speak and act the truth, and to pray that God will bring the world into his kingdom.

The conversion of Constantine to Christianity in the fourth century, however, brought other Christians to accept *the stewardship of power.* Drawing on the long Old Testament tradition of God's gift of coercive power to humans and reflecting on many sayings in the New Testament, they believed that God had placed the sword of justice in their hands, and that they were responsible to use it in order to do right for their neighbors. This tradition seeks to use power as if God were king of the world, and thus to protect God's creatures from evil. When you vote for taxes to support a police force, or bring legal suit against racist or sexist employers, you support this tradition.

Both traditions recognize right wrath. Christian radicals know the prophetic anger born of love when they cry out against war. Christian stewards use force against evil, for love's sake. Yet both need to remember how dangerous even the most righteous anger is. It is crucial to both traditions to listen hard to God through meditation on Scripture, attentiveness to the world, serious prayer, and committed silence. Thus they may share with growing intimacy in God's loving purposes, and not be soured by the sin of anger.

When one has fallen into the sin of anger, how does one repent? Begin by confessing the sin to God. Come to God humbly and honestly, and name the wrong thing you have done and the wrong way your heart is directed. Avoid telling God just how hateful the other person is; he knows. Then ask for God's forgiveness, and for the communion with his love that will enable you to love.

When I sin in anger, I have found it much the best to find a priest and make my confession sacramentally—what my church calls "the rite of reconciliation of a penitent." It is a simple matter of being sorry for one's sin and owning up to it in God's presence, with the help of another Christian who has the authority to give help. In response to my confession, the priest speaks God's word of absolution:

> Our Lord Jesus Christ, who offered himself to be sacrificed for us to the Father, and who conferred power on his Church to forgive sins, absolve you through my ministry by the grace of the Holy Spirit, and restore you in the perfect peace of the Church.

In confession one goes to Jesus' cross, the spring from which God's reconciliation flows. That is where God's wrath is revealed as love for us, and so it is the crucial place to bring our own anger to be forgiven and transformed. Consider also that when one has needed forgiveness and received it, it is a little harder to refuse forgiveness to others. When one acknowledges God as judge and finds him merciful, it is awkward to go on being unmerciful one's self. In fact, a great advantage of confession in dealing with anger is that it implies that one's own self-invented integrity and purposes are not absolute, and that one will no longer defend them in alienation from God and other people. Simply by going to God, one climbs out of one's armor and lets God be the absolute one. Just by seeking out a priest, one moves back into fellowship.

From that center of reconciliation, there are several steps to be taken. One starts by stopping the overt actions that express sinful anger and fuel the spiral: stop the killing and the fights, stop the snide remarks and the backstabbing, stop discriminating. That is harder than it sounds; one's heart can be sneaky, and take revenge at one level while claiming to renounce it at another.

Then comes the next step: the hard discipline of looking at the world from God's perspective, not merely your own. That means learning to see the people at whom you were angry as God sees them. One's most obnoxious neighbor is someone for whom Jesus died. God's salvation reaches to the end of the earth; he means to lead all nations into the New Jerusalem. Enemies and wrongdoers have to be viewed in the light of that eternal future. In particular, if one claims to live in the hope of ultimate pardon by God, one cannot insist that God deny it to others. Christians must not press charges against their enemies on the Last Day. In that court, one simply must not stand against one's neighbor.

Reconciliation may gain further ground by getting to know the people at whom one is angry, learning to honor the good in them, and seeing the world from their angle for a bit. A face-to-face meeting may help. Some years ago, living with my family on a strict budget, our landlord badly cheated us. Three months of prayer did not cool my resentment. I would extinguish the fire of anger several times a day, and immediately find it aflame again. God never required me to deny the truth as I saw it; he only required me to forgive. It was my wife who broke the log-jam. Without my knowledge she invited the landlord to tea, and he had the effrontery to come. When the man ate our bread, however, sitting across from me in the house we rented from him, something in me gave way. I could not feed him and hate him. I was forced to begin to see him whole; there was more to him than the wrong he had done me. He might not even think what he had done was wrong. Perhaps God did not, either. God willed him good; I finally found that I did so too. Letting go of my anger and forgiving him was a gift of sheer grace.

Sometimes we must labor under the cross for a long time, renouncing anger again and again, learning to see as God sees, praying to share in his truth and love. Even so, God forgives freely. But from time to time, God simply gives the gift of reconciliation directly, perfectly, and immediately, just as he sometimes heals people with cancer without making them go through surgery and chemotherapy first. Resurrection sometimes breaks in now, with glory.

Chapter 6

Envy

T he people of ancient Rome feared the "evil eye." A particularly gifted citizen might enjoy good fortune, having served diligently as he climbed the ladder of responsibilities and honors of Roman society. The generous-minded would see that his happiness was a reward for the steady application of his abilities, and be glad for him. Others, however, might begrudge his success as well as his gifts. As he passed such people in the street, they would cast a glance filled with ill will against him. The Romans thought that such a look of peculiar malice, the "evil eye," had power; it carried misfortune and death. One woman could look at another who was blooming with youth and beauty, and her look could carry a hatred which meant to wither the rose. Romans called that look *invidia*. From that word comes our English term, "envy."

We who are the children of the Enlightenment do not believe in the power of the evil eye, but everyone knows what it looks like nonetheless. "If looks could kill...." One can see it at a meeting, in a bar, in a school corridor. For a moment the bland, social mask drops from someone's face. A spark of sour hatred leaps from the eyes. That look does not take its power as much from wanting what the other person has, as from the unbearable fact that the other person has it.

A young woman may win a man's love, and have a friend hate her for it. A toddler may drop his own cookie to grab another child's, just because the other child has one. A scholar may belittle or refute a colleague's insight, simply because she herself did not think of it. In some offices, those who get promoted had best not turn their backs; the knives are sharp. Vestments are no defense. A priest can hate a fellow priest who is eloquent and insightful, or is called to a plum church, or who is simply holy.

Trivial or vicious, envy has the same profile. Envy is resentment of the good another person enjoys, with hatred of the other person for having it. It moves beyond the shallower deadly sins toward something worse: ill will pure and simple, the hatred of good because it is good.

On its more elementary levels, envy may seem like avarice. Someone else has something one lacks: a car or a college acceptance or a good job or a house, hair of a certain color or the ability to sing. Unlike avarice, however, envy does not simply seek to acquire that thing; it resents the other's possession of it. It grudges the fact that someone else should have what it does not; then, as it blossoms, it hates the other person and wishes to destroy their good.

Today on the streets of Washington, young people are killing each other for a pair of shoes or a portable stereo. Yet their rage does not come from having bare feet and wanting shoes; the violence goes far beyond what would be necessary to steal the things. It explodes in response to the feeling of being put down, by the "disrespect" from someone who has what the killer does not. To some extent, the thing coveted still matters—when the police find the body, the shoes or the stereo are gone. But what matters more is that the person who owned them is dead. He elicited the hatred of envy, and was destroyed by it.

As envy grows more profound, it may seek to destroy everything in sheer malice. It does not steal; it breaks and crushes. It hates the good that evokes its own emptiness. Whatever reminds one of the death within must itself die.

Years ago, another pastor's three children would come to visit my own family on vacations now and then. We enjoyed playing with the other children; they were nice. Their family seemed normal, their parents loving and sane. As the years passed, however, all three children took inexplicable bad turns—they fell out with their parents, left school, used and sold heroin. In the end, one of them drifted into prostitution; two joined a particularly vicious gang. Three young people and two parents were destroyed, and there was no explaining it.

Shortly after the family's breakup, the children's aunt died. In her last days she called her sister, the mother of the three. She told her that she had despised her sister's happiness and had resolved to destroy it by corrupting her children. Over the years she had invited the three to her city apartment, in a way that seemed entirely normal. There she treated them royally, far better than their underpaid parents could. She introduced them gradually to her bitterness, to lies about their parents, to adult sex, to the pleasure of drugs—all without a hint to the parents. She told this to her sister as a final act of triumph on her deathbed. That family was destroyed beyond healing. It was not simply that the aunt had wanted a family herself and had tried to steal her sister's. She saw her sister's family with an evil eye, and destroyed it in malice.

Those two aspects of envy—coveting and annihilating—are really one. When humans turn away from God and try to be little gods for themselves, their grasp on divinity is never secure. The vacuum sucks at the center, the worthlessness trembles on the brink of exposure. Envy is emptiness in action.

— The Seat of Envy —

Like anger, envy grows at a deeper level of human life and experience than the sins related to material being. Consequently it is more damaging, and harder to heal. Lust and gluttony begin with ordinary bodily hungers—the desire for sex and food. Sin can distort those desires, cut them away from God and from the rest of human life, spread along the connections to still deeper levels of human being. Yet envy begins its work already at a deeper level.

Human beings are creatures. They are made to be one particular thing by God. That fact has two implications related to envy. One is that humans are dependent. They must receive everything they are and can become from God. They are derivative; they do not exist absolutely of themselves, as God does. Even Carl Sagan did not invent himself. The other implication is that human beings are one thing and not another; their possibilities are finite and limited, unlike God's. Humans cannot live for a thousand years like redwood trees or fly like seagulls or swim like dolphins. Furthermore, each particular human being has an individual face, certain particular gifts and not others, a unique history. Einstein was good at physics and bad at finding his way home in the evening. Each human being is a finite creature.

God blessed his finite creatures, and called them good. To be created is sheer gift. Humans are meant to rejoice in the particular blessing of being chosen, thought out, willed into existence as themselves by God. One begins and ends in relationship, never alone; always saying thank you, and praising the Giver. To accept one's creatureliness brings with it the joy of living relationship with the Creator.

Second, each person's particular self is particular gift, not only as a blessing to one's self, but to glorify God and bless one's neighbors in one's own distinctive way. Each woman or man reflects God's image according to her or his own personal character and gifts. My father-in-law characteristically expressed his version of God's wisdom and love by methodical, prudent planning for his family's future. Someone else will express the same wisdom and love in an utterly different way: through poetry or song. Each is unique, irreplaceable— definite, finite.

Human beings are created to live together, cooperating, taking delight in each other, depending on each other's quite different gifts and goods, and enjoying those gifts in each other. "No man is an island." No one has every gift or grace. Some things have to be enjoyed in our neighbors. Paul's discussion of spiritual gifts in 1 Corinthians 12 underlines this. There is only one Spirit, given to all. But the gifts that Spirit gives to each member of the church are quite distinct. Not all are prophets or apostles or teachers; some heal, some help, some speak in tongues. Because all are one in Christ and share a common life in the Spirit, they have a true communion, a real participation in each other and in each other's gifts. An old New Testament professor of mine had dazzling gifts for scholarship and teaching, but none at all for administration. If he hoped to have a classroom with chalk at the blackboards and lights that worked, someone with the gift of running things had to be around. Paul saw this diversity itself as a wonderful gift: it is an occasion for love. We can delight in each other and depend on each other. What I do not have, you do. That is a ground of shared joy.

The sin of envy is a rebellion against finitude. It begins where all sin does, in separation from God. Perhaps when the serpent in the Garden of Eden tempted our first parents to eat of the fruit of the tree of the knowledge of good and evil, it was in part a temptation to be envious of God.

> The serpent said to the woman,... "God knows that when you eat of it your eyes will be opened, and you will be like God, knowing good and evil." (Gen. 3:4-5)

To want to be like God: not confined to the limited life of a creature, but to have the unlimited possibility of God! Our first parents began to envy the Infinite, and to refuse the finite good that they had been created to be. For the envious children of Eve and Adam, finitude has seemed a condemnation. Cut off from God, we envy God. Different from our neighbor, we envy our neighbor.

We resent deeply that we are not God. To accept being a creature now does not seem like a blessing. We live barely suspended above the abyss of non-being. Some rebel against that, in pride, aggressively denying their finitude, claiming and conquering a universe for themselves. Others welcome the darkness, in the disposition called accidie or sloth, and refuse to live out gladly the fullness of what they are called to be. More will be said about this in the next chapter. But from either response, the refusal to accept one's creation as a finite being produces envy, against God and one's fellows. Proud envy wants to grab and claim all for the self; sad envy wants darkness to claim everything.

At its deepest, envy rejects God. One wants to be self-secure, self-sufficient, omnicompetent. One wants to live forever, live without limits except one's own choice. One wants to be "like God," and cannot. Thus one envies God's life.

That, of course, perverts the relationship. One cannot trust or love or serve someone whom one resents profoundly. The gift of knowing God becomes a bitter reminder of what one is not. Something similar happens to our lives with our neighbors. Other people's gifts become an occasion for reminding me of my own narrow limits. I compare myself to them and feel the fact that I do not have what they do. It hurts. I feel empty and angry. I resent the other person. I may simply want to seize from him what I lack. Or I may destroy what he has, or seek to destroy the person himself, so that he may be as empty as I am.

At times it is the other person's very being that ignites envy. Mary is bright, efficient, and very competent. Jack finds that Mary provokes within him a sense of his own uselessness. He wants to be as good as Mary, and cannot. Instead of enjoying what Mary is by becoming her colleague or friend, the abyss within him responds in malice. It may start simply with Jack's fantasies of putting Mary down, belittling her; that in turn may flower into backbiting and contempt. Jack may go further still, and seek to obstruct Mary's work, even to destroy Mary herself.

Fay Weldon's astonishing novel, *The Life and Loves of a She-Devil*, is a story of envy. One woman, ungainly and unloved, sees her husband being seduced by a beautiful, petite, rich author of bodice-ripping fiction. The wronged woman does not simply seek revenge. Piece by piece, she actually turns herself into the other woman, while displacing and destroying her rival completely. She saps her rival's creative powers while becoming a writer herself. She has plastic surgeons convert her physically into the other woman's twin, as the other woman falls ill, turns pale and ugly. She takes over the other woman's house, occupation, style of life absolutely, and finally wins her man back as her slave. She leaves the other woman nothing except a grave; she has devoured her. Envy has total victory.

There would be another, opposite, way for envy to win, of course. If envy does not boil out at others who provoke it, it may eat away inside like acid. The "she-devil" could have turned the envy within, on herself, and starved or boiled-herself to death.

Envy rejects God's act of creation of finite creatures. It hates looking outside of itself and finding anything that reminds it of its limits, its emptiness. Envy wants it all—or for no one to have anything.

Any social pyramid can be envy's playground. The base of the corporate ladder (or clergy ladder, or football ladder, or

Junior League ladder) is littered with envy's corpses. Furthermore, it is quite possible for a nation or a people, a corporation or a church to be envious. Whole communities can envy others, and go on cultivating it for generations. One of the worst effects of social injustice is the spiral of envy it can generate. The class system in England is fueled by envy. The intractable rivalries between peoples in Ireland and Palestine include a major share of envy—of land, advantages, even of ethnic character.

— Forms of Envy —

There are a number of forms in which this spiritual illness presents itself. One of the simplest is *jealousy*. That is perhaps the least serious form, but the most common. My two teenage daughters were walking down a California street as our family was coming back from the general store. Suddenly the elder of the two bent down to the sidewalk and picked up a ten dollar bill. My wife and I whooped it up and gave her a hug. Then we saw that our younger daughter was standing still, speechless, stunned. Desperately she demanded that her sister share the money with her, or have it taken away. Then she burst into tears. She could not even try to be glad for her sister; she could only feel the ten dollars she herself had *not* found.

My daughter's jealousy started when her sister's good fortune made her feel a lack she had not felt until that moment. She had not known that she did not have ten dollars until her sister did. In jealousy, all one learns from another person's having something is that one does not have it one's self.

Contempt is a somewhat more virulent form of envy. Contempt does not permit itself consciously to feel any lacks. Anything that might raise doubts about one's own full adequacy is simply put down as insignificant. Jock fraternities ignore the inhabitants of sunless library carrels. Some surgeons seem unaware that nurses may be human. Anglo-Saxons have considered Celts as beneath contempt for a millennium and a half, and men have lived in contempt of women for longer than that.

To ignore people, qualities, good things, as unworthy of notice may protect one's own self-absorption and self-worship from conscious threat. The price is the loss of those others, made in God's image, reflecting God's goodness in ways we could not do ourselves. It also has a devastating effect on the people who are the objects of contempt. How many people labor for years under the weight of the memory of a parent's or former spouse's contempt? The effects of racial contempt of whites for blacks are obvious in every city in the United States.

Another guise of envy is *malice*. Malice goes far beyond coveting something good or ignoring it in contempt; malice hates the good and destroys it. One modest way for malice to work is through gossip, "belittling" others. Consider the word itself: to make someone little. How comforting it is to one's bruised self-esteem to let the hot air out of someone else! They shrivel up in one's mind and in the minds of others.

Malice can also be more drastic. It can seek to corrupt or to annihilate anything good, just because it is good. It wills evil for evil's sake. In the Eastern Christian tradition, envy is the archetypical sin, the sin of the devil. Western Christians (following Augustine) have a strong tendency to regard pure evil as impossible, to see evil as parasitic on what is good, a distortion or corruption of a nature fundamentally good in itself. Yet envy can come close to crossing the line by hating the good, pure and simple. Ancient Christians wondered why the devil would seek to involve the human race in his own ruin. Why should he hate us so much? The answer was envy. He had envied the God he could never be, and so he had fallen away in the first place. Unable to harm God directly, he sought to harm him through his creatures. The devil envied the happiness and promise of the young race that enjoyed the relationship with God that he had abandoned. To take everything humans have and to give *nothing* but death in return: that was the bargain he struck with Adam and Eve in the Garden. Our first parents caught their envy from him, and when they were expelled they brought it with them as a legacy to their children. When God accepted Abel's offering but not Cain's, Cain envied his brother and murdered him. Malice has remained a permanent part of the human story.

— Remedies —

Psalm 73 is the story of a man who fell ill from envy, and who was healed. Like many infections, his began with a wound:

> As for me, my feet had nearly slipped;
> > I had almost tripped and fallen;
> Because I envied the proud
> > and saw the prosperity of the wicked.

Rich, healthy, immune from others' struggles, lucky in everything: some people have it all, and use it against others. They enjoy their violence, in open contempt for God. And they get away with it!

> So then, these are the wicked;
> > always at ease, they increase their wealth.
> In vain have I kept my heart clean,
> > and washed my hands in innocence.
> I have been afflicted all day long,
> > and punished every morning.

God is supposed to punish exploiters, not people who are upright. The writer's useless piety made a bitter contrast with the upward mobility of the wicked.

But then he went to God's sanctuary. Perhaps it was a special feast at the Temple, when everyone went; perhaps it was spontaneous. In the Temple was the Ark of the Covenant and other great memorials of God's rescue of Israel from Egypt's arrogant oppression. The worship there constantly recalled God's mighty acts, freely giving his people all they had and all they were. The writer recollected how evanescent good fortune is, apart from God:

> I entered the sanctuary of God
>> and discerned the end of the wicked.
> Surely, you set them in slippery places;
>> you cast them down in ruin....
> Like a dream when one awakens, O Lord,
>> when you arise you will make their image vanish.

Coming into God's presence, the "image" that was tormenting him dwindled. When one envies others, one needs to recognize that they too are finite, derivative, limited. God's presence sets everything else in true perspective. Before him, what are any creatures?

The writer's own blindness left him abashed:

> When my mind became embittered,
>> I was sorely wounded in my heart.
> I was stupid and had no understanding;
>> I was like a brute beast in your presence.

The evil eye—the eye of envy—is so preoccupied with its own darkness and other people's glory that it cannot see God. When it looks up, it sees Someone who transforms everything.

> Yet I am always with you;
>> you hold me by my right hand.
> You will guide me by your counsel,
>> and afterwards receive me with glory.

Whom have I in heaven but you?
and having you I desire nothing upon earth.
Though my flesh and my heart should waste away,
God is the strength of my heart
and my portion for ever.

Healing a soul corroded by envy is no light matter, nor is straightening the spiral of envy within human society. People suck each other dry; only God can fill the void. One can hope for the new heaven and new earth that God will fill so completely no room for envy will be left, but that hope must be rooted in this earth, now. The cross on which Jesus died is the gateway to that new world. Remedies to envy begin with Jesus' cross and resurrection: his death to envy and his resurrection to God's glory.

Since the Garden of Eden, nothingness has for us been embodied in death. In the Genesis story death is the punishment for sin. We who envied God's limitless existence are under sentence to lose our own; that is another reason to envy God, who cannot die. Furthermore, the impending loss of all we have is a fresh motive for envying what others have. Death is the negative incarnation of the abyss within. We can flee it, deny it, or fight against it, but death will claim everything human.

Yet the God whose infinite life we envied did die. In his infinite compassion, God's Son became a human being to share that void, content to take on the narrow, peculiar confines of human life and to be fixed to a narrow cross. God made himself small and shared the nothingness that threatens to devour us when in Jesus he died, lost everything, and was buried in a narrow grave.

That is why the first remedy for envy is to pay attention to God, particularly to God's presence, God's care, and God's promise in the cross. What is there to envy in the broken body of a dead man? If we can turn mind and imagination and heart to him there, the fiery pressure of envy, of other people's full and vibrant being, grows easier.

When Christians go to God's sanctuary, they find Jesus there. Envy encounters there a God eager to share his own life. When God raised Jesus from the dead, it revealed that God brings infinite possibility out of the narrowest limits, and that finite life surrendered to God in trust arrives at endless joy. The way of the cross is to acknowledge one's finitude. The power of resurrection is to transform finitude into blessing. God reverses envy's curse of demanding to be and have everything one's self; he offers the chance to participate in him. Jesus' resurrection is an invitation to open out into God: to see, to trust, to know, to love—as one who is seen, trusted, known, loved. That is like having a spring of life within one's heart. It is a share in God's infinity.

In God's sanctuary one also finds Christ's body, the church. Living together in communion is good exercise against envy. Others have gifts and graces I do not, and we depend on each other for common life. That may pose temptations, but it is also an opportunity. We can share in others' gifts, and bless the Giver. At a parish supper, instead of envying Mrs. Bell's way with collard greens, I can eat them gratefully.

In a daily way, the best remedy for envy is cultivating thankfulness. Envy cannot grow in a thankful heart. The homely discipline of "counting your blessings" really works. How much we have: light, air; the power of thought, the power of love; "our creation, preservation, and all the blessings of this life." At night, do not stop with recollecting the day's sins before God. Name the day's graces, in particular, one by one, and say thank you. We are each filled with goods, not only empty with wants. Thanking God renews the gladness of our first creation.

Chapter 7

Accidie & Pride

He has a Ph.D. from Princeton and wears it effortlessly. The journals he reads are in languages his colleagues can't read, and he and they both know it. He is not generous about their attempts at scholarly articles, when he notices them at all, but that is the prerogative of a star. He enjoys undergraduate teaching and he lectures with panache; a few students hate him, but more follow him around and he seems to enjoy both sorts. It irks him that the college is church-related: he has to go to chapel on ceremonial occasions and put up with a religion department. He is always at his most cutting and disdainful after listening to the chaplain preach. After hearing a "born-again" student hold forth, he convulsed other skeptics by observing that both births had miscarried.

There are a few who have known him for a long time, however, and who remember that he was raised in a Christian family. When he was twelve years old, his father fell ill. He prayed for his father's healing; his father died. After that he had nothing more to do with his parents' god and has dismissed religion as rubbish ever since.

Arrogance is closely linked to despair, the deadly sin of pride to the deadly sin of accidie. Usually called "sloth" nowadays, accidie is a spiritual listlessness or depression, a reluctance and finally a refusal to respond to God. Pride, on the other hand, puts the self in God's place. These, the sixth and seventh deadly sins, are the most dangerous of all. Unlike the other deadly sins, which begin in physical or social life, accidie and pride begin at the center, at our relationship with God. Both stem ultimately from a refusal to live toward God as dependent creatures made in his image.

Traditionally accidie and pride have been treated separately, and they do seem like opposites—accidie as passive shrinking from created existence, pride as its aggrandizement. Yet they are opposed reactions to a single reality, like twin particles of matter and anti-matter spawned by a high-energy nuclear collision. In contrary ways, both accidie and pride react against the gift of created life as God's sons and daughters. They are reversed images of each other, refracted from a single refusal.

Human beings are created. They exist contingently, derivative from God and dependent upon him. In the language of the psalms, people stand on the created earth, between the heavens and the pit of Sheol. They are poised between the abyss of God's infinite, invisible Being and the abyss of not being at all. God invites human beings to know and love him, and thus to share his life—to trust one abyss and only thus to transcend the other.

At the heart of the mystery of sin is our refusal of that invitation, our separation from God. Without God, there is a vacuum at the center of everything. Once we did not exist, and shortly we will die. Even while walking about on the stage of life, one is aware of the darkness of the wings to each side. Unlike God's, human existence is not absolute; we are not the source of our own life. We were meant to live in glad dependence on God's own eternal life. Cut off from God, life is a riddle. Against the fact that the created self is not God and cannot exist from itself, we sketch for ourselves a life on the edge of the void. Such lives usually take one of two forms—

either shrunken into their own nothingness or violently asserting their own life. That is the source of accidie and pride.

To grasp this, one might imagine a totally solitary life, like Robinson Crusoe without Friday. Abandoned forever, without the human relationships in which our thoughts and feelings naturally grow, one might adopt one of two strategies for keeping going. One way—the style of accidie—would be to dampen down one's inner life. Living at a minimum level of mind and heart, letting thoughts and feelings die down, one might stay alive physically for a long time. Alternatively—the style of pride—one could aggressively cultivate the imagination, peopling the mind with its own creatures. One could carry on debates, walk through memories, create an alternative universe within one's self.

The vacuum left by refusing God (far greater and darker) sucks just below the level of human consciousness. Existence as a creature without its creator, as a necessarily God-turned being who has turned away from God, is unnatural. It produces two characteristic contortions. One is to compromise with the nothingness within. You fear the emptiness, and yet it is so easy to give way. You shrink down, claim little, minimize life. Bit by bit, like a sandcastle as the tide comes in, the self agrees to crumble and be washed away. That is the response of accidie. The other is to pile up more and more sand in the castle, faster and faster: to reject the vacuum by absolutizing the self, by extending it and feeding it and defying the void that awaits. That is the response of pride.

Astronomers now think that the frightful mass of a "black hole" pulls anything near it into itself, with gravity so overwhelming that even light cannot escape from its center. As it sucks matter into its maw, some submit passively without a sign. Like accidie, it is already possessed by the dark before it goes down. Other matter, however, vents a last blast of radiation as it is torn apart. Like pride, it throws out a doomed brilliance from the edge.

— Accidie —

Deidre had a cold childhood. She was never quite able to please her parents, never got very much love. She worked hard to win her law degree and does fine work with federal litigation. The salary and the success aren't as exciting any more, and she's a bit bored and lonely. The meat market of singles' bars turns her off; besides, she's in her late thirties and doubts she could compete. Deeper friendships are hard, as she's busy. She was married for eight years to a man who would never fully commit himself to her, never unreservedly love her, and she is not ready for that risk again. As for God, she never thinks much about the god of her childhood religion.

A major job in the Department of Justice is opening, but it would force her beyond her limits as a lawyer. Perhaps it is safer not to hope too much or try too hard. She'll do paperwork tonight, then maybe drink some wine and watch a video.

Deidre has a mild case of accidie: hopelessness, listlessness, refusal to grow. Accidie has often been called "sloth" in western catalogues of deadly sins. One reason to use "accidie," however, is that "sloth" names the disease by one of its least virulent forms, like calling viral pneumonia a cold. In the ascetic tradition, accidie was clearly recognized as one of the greatest dangers to people in monastic life. There are still modern names for attitudes which may be presentations of the disease: laziness, dejection, passive aggressiveness, despair, spiritual depression. The deadly sin itself, however, is at bottom a clearly defined mode of refusing God's call to live as his child; it rejects created existence in the fullness of God's image, preferring nonbeing.

Gregory of Nyssa, the fourth-century mystical theologian, believed that humans are made for infinite growth in God. As we come to know God more truly, we will find the reality of God calling us even further into what seems like darkness.

Any one human being's grasp on God's truth and life is partial; God exceeds our finite knowledge and love of him. Longing for the reality of God, we have to let go, painfully, of our limited, makeshift relationship with God and venture out into something we cannot grasp. Desire for the divine beauty draws us into a light that at first seems like darkness. The soul thus is meant to grow forever, expanding toward God in an infinite trajectory, moving endlessly into new possibility. Accidie refuses that life. Rather than growing into God, it hunkers down, minimizing possibility, choosing death.

My job requires me to hear many sermons. Seminary students, visiting dignitaries, faculty members may preach several times a week in chapel, and I listen, waiting to take my own turn. I have noticed common patterns and themes after a while. Again and again, the sermons of the last fifteen years seem to return to one issue: self-esteem. Again and again, the gospel of the day turns out to say, you matter, you are significant, you are loved. One dogma stands out: God's unconditional acceptance. This pattern also shows up beyond the circles of therapeutic evangelicalism I usually inhabit. The Rev. Jesse Jackson teaches the cry to African American youngsters: "I am somebody!" It is a cry heard from liberation theologians, from electronic fundamentalists, from self-help manuals, from the mainstream pastors of the middle class. You matter, you are accepted just as you are, you are loved: it is good that you exist.

To some critics, this seems like narcissistic self-justification, cosseting words from the chaplains of the me-generation. Yet it may also point to something more. As I write my own sermons, trying to be faithful to the biblical text and yet responsive to the human situations I encounter, I have felt the power of that blind need for affirmation bending my sermon to its shape. From within me, from my people, the hunger arises for an authoritative voice to say: you are somebody, you are valuable, you are worthy, you really exist. Perhaps it is merely self-indulgence, or perhaps the void is closer to the surface these days, a dull advancing emptiness below the lights of the shopping malls.

The scrabbling after a sense of self-worth, of substantial existence, has been obvious in particular people I served as pastor. Among some men I have come to know well, a bottomless dejection underlies their anger and their effervescence. Some women believe they are unlovely and insignificant. Some clergy know they are failures in the deepest sense, paralyzed by their own spiritual mediocrity. Again and again, beneath a person's strengths and gifts and attainments one finds a deep sense of rejection and emptiness, of flimsy and worthless self. The current antinomianism of mainline churches—the fear of condemning or rejecting anything—reflects a whole people terrified of giving any space to the rejection within. No amount of pastoral counseling or inclusive liturgy seems to fill the hole. The therapeutic community's claim that dysfunctional families and sexual abuse are pandemic does not only point to objective social problems; it is itself a sign of a society desperately seeking to account rationally for a despair that is bubbling up through the cracks in the pavement.

Outside the church, entertainments and distractions barely cover a growing boredom. Making money, getting remarried or having affairs, identifying with causes, being swallowed by a job, flitting through pleasures or angers like a hummingbird through fuchsias: all distract one from the darkness a bit better than flipping channels on late-night TV. But they still do not entirely efface the cold tide and the crumbling sand. Ideals and organizations succeed little better; politics and institutional religion smell about the same. There is not much to stand on, hardly anything that gives final dignity to human existence. Beneath the campaigns and markets, under the daily commutes and the mortgages, behind the drugs and distractions, nothingness creeps in like fog.

Some intellectuals cultivate a pose of being at home in the void, like Phillipe Petit coolly self-possessed on a high wire over Niagara. At my alma mater, the philosophy department is coextensive with the department of mathematics—reasonable enough since symbolic logic is their only interest. In the psychology department, behaviorists have undercut Freud; in English and French, deconstructionists ignore the ostensible meaning of literary texts. Professors of religious studies offer a humanist account of religious experience as the projection of social ego. In a pluralist university, nothing much is real.

All this is fertile ground for accidie. Some people will levitate above their unreality for a long time. But others, bit by bit, will stop trying.

Accidie is partial consent to non-being, striking a bargain with insignificance. Its classical progression in monastic life was straightforward. A nun would begin to feel a resistance toward God, a sort of resentful tiredness. She would turn down opportunities to serve or to grow; occasions of grace were ignored or declined. She would turn inward but not to God; she would pull back from relationships, not responding to love, closing her eyes at light, in a spiritual analogue to depression. Her shrinking continued into final despair: the certainty of God's rejection, and her own rejection of any new possibility. One way or another, the end was suicide, though she might go through the motions of religious life with her despair undetected, while her physical life wore on.

A man in his forties, an effective lawyer, has a baby boy who is afflicted by Downs' Syndrome. Anyone would be vulnerable to depression under the burdens that inevitably follow such a diagnosis. Yet his wound is deeper. He blames God; bitterness spreads. He goes to church, he stays on some committees, he cares for his son; but in his heart he is certain that God cannot love him, and his heart pulls back. He goes through the motions of conventional piety until his funeral thirty years later; motions are all they are, until he makes no further motion. He had died much earlier, of accidie.

— Forms of Accidie —

Accidie offers many levels of spiritual disease, not all of them equally virulent. One of the most superficial is common or garden-variety laziness: *sloth*. The teenage boy who does not carry out the garbage or make his bed is making no deep covenant with death; he is just ignoring his duty. The positive good he declines—contributing to an hygienic and orderly environment shared with others—may seem rather abstract to him when the TV or basketball court beckons. Yet in a small way he is on the side of entropy, not new creation. Procrastination of tasks one doesn't like, shirking of responsibilities, comfort blanketing a summons to motion: all start in a simple-minded, self-centered inertia. One prefers one's own little place to movement. Lazy people pull back from the annoying demands that living with others brings.

Sloth soaks deeper as people turn down more opportunities for growth and service. No nights spent at the shelter, no hard study of Scripture, no time spent talking with a bore: it is too much trouble. Church is a drag; stay home with the newspaper or sleep late. That does not mean that everyone who says no to serving on yet another committee is guilty of accidie. Over-commitment and workaholism can themselves be symptoms of the disease, a deliberate distraction from a call to the real journey. If one is locked into constant doing, one may never have to pay much attention to the voice within.

One obvious case of sloth is the eagerness of many Christians to endorse the idea of spiritual discipline alongside their disinclination actually to do anything. George Gallup has recently documented this phenomenon in a study of the Episcopal Church, and it is borne out for other churches as well. Almost everyone knows that daily prayer and Bible study are "good things," but remarkably few actually undertake them. God comes near, offering to open doors to deeper understanding and expanded life; many of us disable the doorbell and go back to bed. Painful self-examination might lead to penitence, the practice of humble service could deepen love, patient prayer would open knowledge. Yet in relation to the abyss of God, sloth prefers to keep sensible limits.

It is so much easier *not* to respond, to coast through French class and never become fluent, to stop writing to one's relatives or going to see them and so be spared the effort and aggravation that being a family requires. The Aristotelian tradition, running through Thomas Aquinas and Richard Hooker, considered sloth the fundamental sin of the intellect. Thinking hard and critically is painful; it is easier to stay warmly dressed in conventional wisdom.

To begin to live toward the full possibility of growing into the stature for which humans are made requires one to turn away from the lower comforts of one's own inertia. It requires one to answer God's voice in faith. Sloth says, thanks, not right now. The lazy servant in Matthew 25, who was given one talent to invest but buried it in the ground, in the end lost everything.

Another way to sin by accidie is to empty out one's self in idol worship rather than growing toward God, seeking significance in some other human being or cause or circumstance. A father may simply live for his daughter, even embezzle money so that everything will be perfect for her, and never say no to her in anything. She is effectively his god, and he defines his existence as service to her. On the other hand, women in particular have felt themselves called to sacrifice and efface themselves, not so that God's kingdom might dawn, but in mute identification with their male lords. That sort of *self-abdication* offers a temporary refuge both from God and from the nothingness that stalks created life. Oppression may join a devil's dance with idolatry. As the void comes closer to the surface of the common life, the dance is speeding up.

A story:

> *Ellen has spent her life as a good Christian, full of good works, regular in all duties. She has a warm heart; a deep interior sense of God's presence has flowered gradually during years of prayer. Five years ago, she began to feel that she needed more guidance from God regarding the direction of her life in the future. She asked for it earnestly and humbly. Instead of getting it, the sense of God's presence itself began to vanish. Like the tide going out, it left a wan, flat expanse stretching out without relief. She has not felt God's movement within her for years now; she feels stagnant and cold within. Finally, she felt that going on with prayer was just banging her head against a wall. She has stopped seeking and asking for anything.*

The silence of God is hard to bear. The abyss is undisguised. One feels abandoned, that struggle is pointless, that love has nothing to nourish it and cannot grow. I do not think anyone really understands the desert, yet it is crucial to avoid confusing it with sin. It was the Spirit, after all, who drove Jesus into the wilderness. The great teachers of prayer all say that when the normal supports of faith are taken away and there is no sign of God, one may grow most deeply toward God.

Yet if the desert is a place of pilgrimage, it is also a place of temptation. Teresa of Avila spent years in which her prayer seemed to reach nowhere and produce nothing, and so she made what she called the greatest and most dangerous mistake of her life: she gave up mental prayer. That is the attack of accidie: not the dryness itself, but leaving the path in despair of finding living water.

The fruit of accidie, in the end, is *despair*. In its terminal form, it finally rejects God's new possibility. It rules out grace, shuts any opening to the divine life.

The traditional example of despair is Judas. Medieval preachers pointed out that Peter had sinned almost as greatly by denying Christ as Judas had by betraying him. Could not Judas have repented? God will forgive any sin. In fact, they pointed out, Judas even followed the steps of repentance: he confessed his sin to the priests ("I have betrayed innocent blood") and made restitution (flinging back the thirty pieces of silver). But Judas, unlike Peter, did not stay with the other disciples and open himself to God's mercy. Still rejecting, still withdrawn, certain of his damnation, he went out and hanged himself. Accidie has its full effect when one puts oneself intentionally beyond the reach of God's mercy.

Spiritual withdrawal and depression often start with dishonest prayer, refusing to raise some issue with God, rejecting a summons, getting tired of God's silence and walking away. It is natural enough to feel hurt or rejected by God, when disaster leaves wounds, or if one's spiritual aspirations are simply left hanging for years. Yet those might be taken as invitations to the cross, to die to one's own self in a new way and live in sheer dependence on God even in the dark. Accidie rejects that invitation. It chooses to live and die on the margins of its own nothingness rather than launch out further into the abyss of God. It leaves the self independent from God and in control, even at the price of self-minimization. Here one can see how closely related accidie is to pride. Those who bargain with nothingness can avoid surrender to God.

— Pride —

Pride fills the history books. The armies of Alexander the Great left the whole world prostrate before him, and he wept that there was no more to conquer. American "robber barons" subdued a continent to their economic will and then named colleges after themselves with the profits. Yet not everyone infected with pride leaves such memorials. Who remembers my seventh-grade baseball coach, screaming himself purple at some underling who questioned his judgment?

The seventh deadly sin is pride: putting one's self in God's place, above everything and everyone. Rather than depend on God as a creature, pride makes the self absolute. Much of the Western tradition has regarded pride as the root of all the other vices; it is the archetypical sin, the sin of the devil. In John Milton's *Paradise Lost*, Satan vaunted himself against God magnificently, playing out the self-assertion that horrified (and attracted) the Puritans most. In recent years in America, however, self-aggrandizement has become a cultural virtue. A magazine for women is named *Self*; an American journalist calls America the most important fact of the whole millennium; in politics and on the gridiron, the chant goes up: "We're number one!"

Not that God seeks false humility:

> When I look at your heavens, the work of your fingers,
> > the moon and the stars that you have established;
> what are human beings that you are mindful of them,
> > mortals that you care for them?

> Yet you have made them a little lower than God,
> > and crowned them with glory and honor.
> You have given them dominion over the
> > works of your hands;
> > You have put all things under their feet. (Ps. 8)

God delights in particular things. Every snowflake, every goldfinch, every single creature is itself. Each human face, each human intelligence has its own shape, each people and nation its own character. If there is a San Francisco in heaven, it will not be an imitation of Jerusalem but a more perfect San Francisco. The fog will be even cooler and the salt air cleaner, the sun brighter, the swoop of the hills and the gulls and the peoples' lives even wilder.

In creating humans, God made creatures who are self-conscious. We are aware of being ourselves. We can remember and recollect ourselves, we can know and even relate to ourselves. Knowing ourselves goes together with knowing God and neighbor, and loving them. Augustine, who was entranced by the mystery of the human self, thought that human nature is essentially receptive, naturally determined by relationship. It must love and choose what it will take into itself; what becomes of it depends on that choice. We are created good, but empty; something must fill us. Those who are filled with God are whole, "perfect," truly themselves.

For a humanity lurching between accidie and pride, it is sometimes difficult to understand the right joy of created beings in God and thus their right joy in their own existence. Perhaps Luke's story of the angel Gabriel's good news to Mary may help illustrate it. When Mary was told that she was so greatly loved and favored by God, she did not try to deny it, but rejoiced:

> For behold from henceforth
>   all generations shall call me blessed;
> for he that is mighty has magnified me.

There is no sign in her of the weak personality that some set as opposite to pride; whatever portrait of Mary emerges from the gospels, it is not one of a compliant woman. Yet it is clear where her joy in her existence sprang from, and where her attention was focused. She became great in God's greatness. It was God's name that was holy, and it was because of God's blessing that she would be called blessed. The glory of humans is to be lit up by God's glory and so to be free.

Pride turns to self, away from God. Pride insists on being its own light. Like accidie, it rejects the status of creature, but takes the opposite tack. On the brink between the abyss of God and the abyss of non-being, accidie accepts a bargain with nothingness; pride asserts divine absoluteness for itself.

—— Forms of Pride ——

Vanity is one way that pride shows up. Holding the center of attention—one's own and others'—is almost the meaning of life to some of us. Body-builders sculpt their flesh, intent on the mirror as they lift weights. A priest offers the perfect liturgy, every tone and gesture immaculate, the congregation serving as mirror. Cosmeticians and cosmetic surgeons sell physical beauty to millions.

Of course, a due regard to one's appearance is a sign of normal health; a cat that looks dirty and unkempt is sick. Yet fixation on one's appearance is a sign of illness, too. If one is thinking about how one looks, one is not attending to the business at hand. Genuinely happy people look genuinely wonderful, but their beauty does not come from looking at themselves. Mirrors add nothing to what they reflect.

Narcissism can go further than mere appearances, however. One can also create one's self in whatever image one likes. People develop a persona or a life-style as a work of art, clipped and tightly wired like a bonsai tree or flaming out in extravagance. In local high schools, kids work hard to make themselves the crispest preppie, the coolest homeboy student athlete, the hottest babe. In religious circles, the vogue of spirituality sometimes shimmers with narcissism. "Make yourself what you will, a Teresa or a Francis. You can be anything you want to be!" Yet sometimes our contrived selves seem as flat as the pages of the magazines they come from.

In fact, the self is God's creation. Obviously we do help shape ourselves, but death and resurrection await us. "It doth not yet appear what we shall be"—God's future for the self is beyond the control of pride. Ironically, people who leave their creation to God seem to end up remarkably substantial people and quite different from each other. Thomas Aquinas' incisive, balanced architecture of mind was utterly different from Julian of Norwich's deep, layered dialogue with Christ. Lyman Beecher preached fiery, hyperactive sermons to evangelize America; Harriette Beecher Stowe, his daughter, wrote novels to reshape America's moral imagination. Each meant to be and do what God willed, and yet were as far from uniform plaster casts of each other as possible.

Pride also shows up in its effects on one's relation with other creatures. For the self-centered, other people do not easily make an impression; nothing besides the self has very much reality. The husband who expects his wife to attend to his creature comforts and puts up with her prattle only because he can filter it out is really married to himself. When I was growing up, an elderly relative occasionally made a pontifical visitation to our home. When she entered my mother's kitchen, it was of course reordered her way. The children paid her court, if they knew what was good for them. She was not a tyrant, exactly, simply the hub of reality.

Our ambition makes the people around us into building blocks. Getting my vision realized because it is mine, achieving my goals, whether or not they serve anyone else, winning the position I want regardless of others' merit: ambition vaults me into first place. That is not a sport restricted to individuals; families, tribes, nation-states, religious movements have all served ambition's turn. Each Benedictine monk, for example, took vows that required humility and self-abnegation as an individual. During the Middle Ages, however, that seldom restrained monks from trumpeting the glory of their patron St. Benedict and of their house and order against all competition. No one ever cultivated a prouder humility than a Spiritual Franciscan against all the rest of the church, unless it was an orthodox Calvinist.

Another style of social pride is domination. Pride does not need neighbors except as mirrors or as slaves. One's own truth is what is true, one's own will is what is right, and others must be made to fall into line. Hitler was *der Führer,* the Leader, whose vision of an Aryan Europe ruled Germany absolutely. Stalin, Mao, Pol Pot moved "the masses" where they chose, made them or unmade them as they liked. Domestic tyrants can do much the same, or bullies on playgrounds. One of the greatest gifts I had from my childhood was that my parents did not dominate me; they tried honestly to bring me up "in the nurture and admonition of the Lord." They respected God first, and thus my upbringing was not a matter of them creating me as an icon of themselves. God's knowledge of me, God's purposes toward me, were what mattered. That left my parents free to be confident in their own authority, free to make mistakes, free to see me grow in ways they had not foreseen—free to let me be real, in relation to God and thus to them. That gift of true freedom pride cannot give.

It is in relation to God, of course, that pride—here often called "spiritual pride"—takes its most vicious turn. The self-deification that is implicit in other forms of pride here becomes explicit. The self is god.

Some atheists are proud in this way. This is not to say that some have not done their thinking in good conscience, driven to their conclusion with great pain. Yet their presumption—almost universally shared in modern times—is that they can judge the question of God justly. The view, however, that the human intellect is a neutral arbiter of truth, disinterested and objective, has not withstood criticism very well. Human beings are never disinterested where God is concerned; they are in his image on one hand, and implicated in an active misrelation with him on the other. There can be no intellectual neutrality on the question of God. For a contingent being to consider and reject God is pride.

Pride can work equally well, however, with vigorous belief in God's existence. Creeds make fine weapons. One need only take the truth as one's own possession, rather than God's. The church has seen many highly sanctified people who wanted their names to be holy, and their own sacred will to be done on earth.

Moralists list many sub-categories of spiritual pride. Impenitence denies guilt, or, if it cannot, is too proud to come to God for forgiveness. Presumption makes its own way without seeking help from God—who needs a crutch? Hypocrisy sets (and enforces) the highest moral and spiritual standards for others, substituting itself for God as teacher and judge. Sacrilege appropriates holy things and holy words and uses them for its own purposes, not God's. Blasphemy overtly assaults God.

Pride in all its forms seems bold, assertive, strong. Yet it has literally nothing to back it up. Turned away from God, the darkness is very deep. Pride huddles over its own little campfire, blinded to the stars in the black heavens. Staring into the small flame, it almost succeeds in forgetting how few sticks are left to keep the fire going.

— Accidie, Pride, and the Deadly Sins —

Accidie and pride are opposite twins, spinning out in contrary directions from their shared origin. Both refuse God. Both are fixated on the self: one shrinks it, the other inflates it. Both are acts of denial, refusing to live by the reality of God and his gift of created life.

Accidie and pride take root at the very foundation of human life, and inevitably flavor everything that grows out of that root. As a result, each imparts a characteristic style to the other sins it occasions. A person who has a bent toward accidie may practice other deadly sins with a surly, rejective, self-diminishing tone. Someone whose basic style is more prideful may shape other sins in a dominating, self-aggrandizing way.

Lust is a case in point. For accidie, God's call into union with Christ in celibacy or through one's spouse demands too much faith. Lifelong, unreserved sexual commitment would mean accepting finitude and living in hope. Trivial sex may distract one from the abyss, like any other entertainment. Alternatively, suppressing sexuality altogether might make even fewer demands. Shrunken marriages and bitter celibates are the detritus of accidie.

There is another cruel twist that accidie can give to sexual life. Despair and self-contempt can lead people to use sex as a sort of sacrament of their own worthlessness. One can accept sexual domination as one's due. Some people cling to an overtly degrading relationship as if it were all that could validate their existence. Accidie consents to put another human in God's place, and to be swallowed up in that relationship. At least it keeps the final night at bay.

Pride, in contrast, uses sex in any way that serves its self. It can use bodies like Kleenex, but longer-term relationships offer plenty of room for pride, too. Making love skillfully can be a powerful form of self-expression and self-assertion analogous to art. Everyone knows marriages that are fields of battle, each spouse seeking to dominate the other. Glamorous young women who marry rich older men are currently called "trophy wives"; both satisfy pride their own way.

Gluttony too may show the distinctive twists of accidie and pride. In accidie, the vacuum at the center of life demands to be fed; despair's hunger is not a positive desire for good things, but a gaping hole that swallows and is never satisfied. Misery loves its little comforts. If the emptiness comes closer to the surface, one can make a bargain with death in the form of anorexic or bulimic behavior. Refusing to eat (or to digest) is a last refuge for a person left powerless in the void. Yet it makes common cause with that void, leaving stomach and soul both empty.

Pride has its own ways to exploit gluttony. Church potluck dinners can be great times of personal competition for cooks: whose chicken divan is gone and whose has barely been tasted tells a tale. Ostentation in food is a traditional expression of an ostentatious ego. Yet proud gluttony is marked chiefly by eating without sharing and without thanksgiving. The person (or nation) that eats first and most, without inviting others to the table, is making it clear who matters most.

Avarice gets different spins from accidie and pride. The hamster's wheel of getting and spending in our culture turns in part by despair. One seeks distractions, security, something solid and palpable, and may try to find it in things. The inner self may be flimsy, but a diversified portfolio or a Range Rover is built to last. The dispirited can buy spirit. Accidie can feed the darkness with things, while pride uses them to insulate the ego. In antiquity, a king who was a real king built great buildings, even whole cities; the first Christian emperor aptly had his trophy city named after himself—Constantinople. In the Middle Ages, the gentry scrambled for land to provide their status. The display of silver in their halls—masses of plate: cups and platters and flagons and bowls—drove the point home to other gentry neighbors. Since then, egos have not changed much: just some of their ornaments. But pride can go further. Things can be used to dominate others, to buy compliance and extort obedience. Wealth means power, and pride knows how to use it.

— Remedies —

Pride and accidie are sins of the center: both refuse to live toward God. Balancing on the edge between God and nothingness, pride swells itself up and accidie cringes. It makes obvious sense to fear the abyss of nonbeing on one side. Its horror usually exceeds its attraction, until accidie is very far advanced or pride meets its final limit. But why the horror of the other side, of God? To understand God's remedy for the sins of the center, it might help to consider that difficulty.

There is no more difficult mystery to Christians than why we shy away from God. God is infinite light and goodness. Why refuse him? Why prefer derivative lights and secondary goods, or choose darkness and evil, when one might live with the source of all good? But we do flee God. Not only accidie and pride, but all other sins, are the means of that flight. The saints have given many answers to these questions: that we wish to be god ourselves, that lesser goods are more comprehensible and accessible, that we do not know God well enough to love him. Yet there is still another reason.

When God came down in fire on Mt. Sinai, Moses hid in the cleft of the rock and only dared to look on God's back. That was not because he wished to hide guilt. It was because of the weight of God's being, the abyss of his glory. "You shall not look upon my face and live." Isaiah did not quail before God enthroned in the Temple only because of his own uncleanness, but because of the One whom he saw. Even the seraphs covered their faces. God is too much for created beings. To face him directly is to confront something exceeding us so greatly that it may even seem like nothing. We do not see. We do not understand. Overwhelming our senses, slipping through our thick fingers, God escapes our grasp. God's light is too bright for our eyes—that is why the Holy of Holies seemed pitch dark to the High Priest who entered it to make atonement.

Yet if Jesus is who the church claims he is, then in him God comes in a way we can receive him. Thus he is the remedy for the sins of the center. Accidie and pride keep their hold on some people because they exclude God from the center, but also because they are fearful or disoriented when God does intrude. Christ is the culmination of God's long work to reenter the heart of human life. God's glory had always been figured in the richness and beauty of the created order. His character could be recognized in the Torah; God was audible in the sharp call of the prophets. Yet in Jesus God became tangible, the uncreated light visible. Jesus is God's presence and God's will, embodied in real human hands that could touch and heal, and be transfixed by nails. To accidie he is God made small enough to enter the narrowest and flimsiest of our hiding places from life. To pride he is God's own integrity of Being, accessible and non-threatening, offering itself as a free gift. He opens a way to enter the abyss of God's love.

Yet the remedy Jesus offers means being willing to accept what he has to give. Even when the invitation is clear, many reject God because, in the style of pride, they regard dependence as demeaning, or, in accidie, they are timid about accepting the gift of full existence. Serious meditation on Jesus as the church understands him, however, may counter both that shame and that timidity. The Son perpetually receives all that he has and all that he is from the Father. The Being of the Second Person is derivative from the First; as God, Jesus is begotten by, derives from, is generated by the Father. As the Nicene Creed puts it, he is "God *from God,* light *from light,* true God *from true God."* If that is true about the life of the Triune God, then dependence is grounded in the nature of things. For a tree to be rooted in the earth is no prison; for God's children to be utterly dependent on God means joy, as it does for Jesus, who shares his Sonship with us.

Accidie has no trouble with dependence; what it has a hard time believing is that God's love intends human beings really *to be.* Yet the creed also teaches that the Son is fully God: *"God from God, light from light, true God from true God, of one and the same Being* as the Father." The Second Person subsists as the full, complete stamp of the Father's whole person. The

Son's being is undiminished, infinite, perfect. That he receives his glory from the Father and refers it back to him does not mean that it is not his. For those who share Jesus' life, there is no reason at all to be timid about that life, to minimize it or to be shy about rejoicing in it. We are created to be the daughters and sons of the living God; God means us really *to be* in his image.

Pride needs to follow Jesus through the gospels, to learn that dependence and derivative existence is good when the dependence is upon God. Accidie needs to follow Jesus through the gospels into the resurrection, to taste and see that God is good—good for us. To the Samaritan woman at the well, Jesus promised:

> Everyone who drinks of this water will be thirsty again, but those who drink of the water that I will give them will never be thirsty. The water that I will give will become in them a spring of water gushing up to eternal life. (John 4:13-14)

When the monks at Rievaulx gathered daily in the abbey church, they came knowing accidie and pride as close companions. The brother whose heart seemed dead and who did not respond to love, the prior who guarded his eminence jealously, the ascetic who thought himself holiest of all: they were familiar characters. Aelred, their abbot, left behind a long prayer in which he asked God to free his heart from both sins so that he might serve his brothers better. In that prayer, it was specifically to Jesus that he turned: Jesus' humility, Jesus' glory. Every day he and the whole community came to that center in the Eucharist, in extended, searching meditation on their Lord, in concrete work and life together in community.

The heart of the Eucharist is Jesus' presence in his death and resurrection. Pride finds forgiveness in Jesus' self-emptying in death, and finds too that Jesus opened the trail it must follow:

Let the same mind be in you that was in Christ Jesus, who, though he was in the form of God, did not count equality with God as something to be exploited, but emptied himself, taking the form of a slave, being born in human likeness. And being found in human form, he humbled himself and became obedient to the point of death—even death on a cross. (Phil. 2:5-11)

Jesus himself said: "If anyone would be my disciple, let him deny himself, and take up his cross, and follow me." Even when I am stinging with an insult to my vanity, or sick at soul with my preening self-consciousness, I can join the line going up to communion, be given a free share in Jesus' selflessness, and summoned to his way of humility.

Accidie is invited to a resurrection in communion with Christ:

Those who eat my flesh and drink my blood abide in me, and I in them. Just as the living Father sent me, and I live because of the Father, so whoever eats me will live because of me. (John 6:54-57)

God's own life draws very close, very gently. If any door is cracked, any window unlocked, hope may steal in.

For people who resolutely keep all doors locked and the blinds pulled, no healing may come to accidie and pride. Yet sometimes Christ comes through locked doors. The most effective means out of pride into reality, I think, are not the disciplines one chooses but the humiliations God sends. Medieval spiritual directors sometimes considered whether God might not allow some of his prouder children to fall into gross sins, simply to disclose the deep disease within and bring a more profound repentance. Augustine acknowledged that his noble, philosophical mind never fully turned to God until he found that he could not give up sex. Perhaps the very intractability of spiritual vanity, wearily struggled with for many years, teaches one to give up on self-creation and wait for God. Sudden events—a death, a loss of a job, a failure—may bring proud people to their knees.

Accidie, too, sometimes responds to direct intervention. Someone may sit down in love and open one's grief directly. A sudden epiphany may change everything. The poet George Herbert was on the verge of throwing over the obedience to God which, he had concluded, was completely fruitless, when love found him:

> Who would have thought my shrivel'd heart
> Could have recover'd greennesse? It was gone
>   Quite under ground; as flowers depart
> To see their mother-root, when they have blown;
>   Where they together
>   All the hard weather,
> Dead to the world, keep house unknown....
>
>   And now in age I bud again,
> After so many deaths I live and write;
>   I once more smell the dew and rain,
> And relish versing: O my only light,
>   It cannot be
>   That I am he,
> On whom thy tempests fell all night.

For most people, perhaps, accidie and pride are not so much terminal diseases dramatically cured as they are chronic conditions. They are so deeply rooted in our life, so implicated in the way each of us deals with reality, that they cannot be wholly eliminated in this life. With some weeds, the whole lawn would have to be killed to get rid of them entirely. Waiting patiently in faith is not the smallest act of hope and humility.

To live by faith means, at times, to continue living toward God even when one's feelings run entirely contrary, when all one's heart can see is barrenness. One of the worst effects of temptations to accidie is that prayer seems wholly unrewarded. One of the most important gifts of the Holy Spirit is *perseverance*. Faith is not a matter of feelings. It is a direction of being, toward God, who is at times wholly invisible. The desert monks and nuns prescribed hard manual labor for their friends who suffered from accidie, since bodies have everything to do with spirits. But chiefly they encouraged them to go on praying, not to give up seeking the Holy Spirit, whom the creed calls Life-giver. Jesus made that point in the parable of the widow who nagged the unjust judge ceaselessly until he finally did right by her: one "ought always to pray and never lose heart."

Perseverance is also crucial with chronic pride. I like to pick blackberries, in dense wild patches where the canes grow well over my head. If I am ever to get back out onto the road with a full pail in my hand, a good stick has to be in the other one to push trailing branches aside and pull off the thorny ropes that entangle me at every step. In the battle to get out of pride's thicket, prayer is that stick. One constantly makes the act of turning from self to God. The hard work of deliberate praise, systematically acknowledging who and what God is, can make some headway against self-praise. Long discipline in the prayer of silence, a silence of heart and mind as well as of voice, helps calm the racket of self-fascination. Daily confession of sin sums up the hourly turnings from proud thoughts and words. Intercession turns one's love toward other people.

The monks of Rievaulx came to communion, they meditated, they prayed without ceasing. But Aelred was also deeply interested in the healing effect of life in Christian community. The daily round of living with other people offers plenty of occasions for accidie or pride, but remedies too. It helps to be among other people in the church rather than self-isolated. When my routine intercessions chance upon a colleague who has thwarted some project of mine, my shield of arrogance may at least get dented. When I feel that the bottom has dropped out of my faith, others can carry me for a while until I can walk again. When an old deaf lady needs a ride to church, I have to set aside my great insights or kick myself out of my gloom and go start up the car. Making sandwiches for hungry people in the neighborhood, and handing them out, does not bring much glory. Neither does counting the collection or stacking chairs, or calling on a sick friend, or spending time reading to one's children, or working honestly at one's job. Concrete, simple, humble deeds disclose the simple reality of other people, however. That can be humbling and encouraging, if only because Christ is sometimes visible in them. In a community gathered around the cross and resurrection, ordinary life helps cement the new center which God is forming in the place of accidie and pride.

Chapter 8

Repentance

C hristianity once possessed a diverse, flexible vo-cabulary for naming the powers that separate us from God. In our present culture, however, "sin" has come to mean little more than half-delicious guilt after a little sexual dalliance or a slice of chocolate cake. Our pilgrimage through the seven deadly sins has offered a different perspective, one that insists that God's goodness is woven through the whole fabric of human life—and so too are the threads of human refusal. From the center of Jesus' cross, we have followed the pattern of God's goodness and human sin through food and sex and property, through the social ability to guard one's integrity and appreciate others' goods, to the divine gift of glad existence as God's creature. A world that considers God as no more than a private sentiment has forgotten how to recognize the power of sin on every level of its common life. That not only blinds it to grave dangers, it stops up the springs of new possibility. When we learn how to name sin, however, we move toward fresh encounter with God on every side.

That was the original purpose of the list of the seven deadly sins. In the Middle Ages, for example, the list served as an aid for a Christian's Easter confession. Throughout Christendom, the whole community was required once yearly to face sin and reconcile with God and each other. In any given village, everyone was expected to undertake a thorough self-examination with the help of the parish priest in order to expose the damage that spiritual disease had done them that year. They were to review each of the sins in turn, looking for signs of evil dispositions in their heart and recalling the wrong acts those dispositions had produced.

In most communities, each of the deadly sins was likely to be active in one person or another. Perhaps gluttony had worked the miller so well on Saturday nights that he was too hung over to make it to church some Sundays. Lust might have moved the miller's outwardly complacent wife to take a little surreptitious comfort with the cooper's son. Avarice could have sharpened the bailiff's pencil when taxes were due. The long-standing anger between the Smith brothers might have blown white hot when their father died and only the elder could inherit the forge. Perhaps the brewer bitterly envied her neighbor, who had five cows, so that she secretly prayed they would die. The parson, aware of much of this, might well have slipped into accidie, doubting that even God could soften the stony hearts of the parish. It might have been the bishop, however, who set the leading example of pride, when one day he rode through the village with his forty mounted escorts and would not soil his feet in the muddy lane to say mass or confirm the children.

The seven deadly sins are always busily at work in Christians and their world, whether in the thirteenth century or the twentieth. But once one can see them and name them, what is to be done about them?

The medieval church's answer was that people should take the three steps of repentance: contrition, confession, and satisfaction. Contrition meant being sorry for the sin; confession meant opening the sin to God and receiving forgiveness; satisfaction meant struggling to undo the continuing effects of the sin. Of course all that was to be done in and through the ministries and sacraments of the church.

As centuries rolled by, the systems that the church developed to foster the three steps of repentance became enormously complicated, expensive, and litigious. The Reformation was a massive reaction against them as cruel and exploitative on every level. Yet rightly understood, the three steps in themselves remain a helpful way of responding to sin.

— Contrition: Being Sorry —

The first step of repentance is contrition: being sorry for sin. It means grief for the attitudes and behaviors that run counter to relationship with God, and turning from them to God. The relationship with God is the key.

Some years ago, James decided to become my friend. I am not much good at friendship with other men my age, but he kept on trying and in the end won through. Sometimes, however, I still pull into my shell and shut him out. When I realize that I have hurt James, I am really sorry. Our friendship matters to me, and he himself matters even more. The sorrow I feel—regret, grief, guilt, hope for renewed friendship and restored damage—is contrition. Contrition is based on relationship. To be sorry for sin implies being sorry toward those you have offended and hoping to renew the relationship.

At the center of all relationships is oneness with God, just as the heart of sin is estrangement from God. When the Holy Spirit moves within a relationship strained by sin, the person awakens and is sorry. I am close to a teenager who recently fell in love with a young woman from a neighboring church. He had been the sort of person who could knock over someone else in passing and never notice, who had never in his life put down a toilet seat for the next user. Yet I saw him just after he had accidentally bumped his chair into hers and cut her hand. He was stunned that he had hurt her, mute with grief. People who love learn what it means to be sorry. The relationship God has with us is alive, true, real. The clearer that is, the more lifegiving our baptism, the more painfully aware we become of our flights and deceptions.

That in part is why God is not always an easy companion. Of course God's love is not contingent on our good behavior. If it had been, the church would never even have reached the first Pentecost. Yet in the long run God's faithfulness reveals our compromises and betrayals, and that is uncomfortable. In one area after another, on level following level, God's light shines on half-perjured loyalty, squalid motives, dubious actions. The very fact that God accepts and loves us as we are creates unease: God is so good, and we are not, very. In relationship with God, awareness of sin creates sorrow.

Baptism is God's gift of relationship with Jesus Christ, and in particular with Jesus' death and resurrection. In Jesus God took initiative to reconcile everyone to himself. In baptism one accepts that reconciliation and enters into a friendship that God has created and promises to maintain. A crucial part of contrition, therefore, is trusting that promise. James has been a steady, faithful friend to me, even when I have hampered things. When I am sorry for wronging him, that sorrow is given the right direction by my trust that he will want to go on being my friend. So all the more with God. All of the great penitential psalms cry out to God, trusting in his commitment to his children:

> Have mercy on me, O God,
> *according to your steadfast love;*
> *according to your abundant mercy*
> blot out my transgressions. (Ps. 51)

"We love because he first loved us." Contrition for sin implies faith that God will keep the commitment he made to us in Jesus.

When I grow sorry that I have ignored James, in a sense the relationship is already restored, at least in me. It was my lack of commitment that strained things. My sorrow comes from a renewed commitment; if I didn't miss James, I wouldn't be sorry. Alienation from God is the heart of sin; being sorry for it is already a movement back toward relationship.

— Confession: Naming Sin —

If I forget to pick up the dry cleaning and so leave my wife without her dress an hour before we have to go out, it is important that I go beyond feeling regretful and actually say something to her about it. In restoring a damaged relationship, one needs to own up to what one did to damage it. Actually naming the wrong and saying one is sorry does not only help others with their job of forgiving, it changes the reality for one's self by making repentance objective. When you *say* you are sorry and name what you are sorry for, it gets it out into the open, no longer half-cherished, covered by defensiveness and equivocation. Confession risks putting weight on the relationship, in vulnerability and trust.

God does not need help with forgiveness; we, however, do. We need to make our renewal of relationship with God explicit by naming our sin and asking for forgiveness.

If we say that we have no sin, we deceive ourselves, and the truth is not in us. If we confess our sins, he who is faithful and just will forgive us our sins and cleanse us from all unrighteousness. (1 John 1:8-9)

As we turn to Christ in the traditional liturgy of baptism, we explicitly renounce evil. Christians who confess their sins to God are simply renewing that renunciation, as a basic part of their baptismal relationship with him.

The churches have discovered a wide variety of ways to confess their sin throughout their history. The liturgies of the Episcopal Church almost all include a corporate confession of sin, some very brief, others going into considerable detail, as in the liturgies for Ash Wednesday and Good Friday. Sacramental confession to a priest is always available and often most helpful in opening particularly nasty or troubling sin to God. Personal confession to God, in the strict privacy of one's heart, is open to anyone anywhere; Jesus, our great high priest, hears confessions at all hours.

Yet naming our sins has its difficulties. The traditional language of sin is rich and many-sided, offering dozens of alternative approaches; the seven deadly sins is only one. Yet sometimes no name quite fits what needs saying. Sin may be subtle, ambiguous, unclear. Even if we do find words to speak to God, we may not be confident that we really understands what we are saying, fully remember all we need to say, truly grasp the depths beneath the names. Any speech to God drives language to the very edge of its potency.

Words need not be perfect in order to do what needs doing, particularly when they are spoken in an ongoing, living relationship. When I call my daughter Libby to supper, her bare name bellowed up the staircase does not fully evoke the depths of her spirit. Nor does the mere word "supper" tell her anything about the chicken cacciatore awaiting her, or whether she will have to face zucchini again. Yet "Libby! Supper!" does get her to the table. When we confess sin to God, we do well to be humble about the adequacy of what we say. Yet that is no reason not to speak the truth as best we can. The words are spoken to God as concrete signs of a renewed relationship with him, not as acts of mastery over our inner lives. Part of the point of making confession is to turn away from pretensions to perfect adequacy or from the silence of despair, and to trust God enough to risk speaking to him, even with poor words. Paul thought that God would help us:

> Likewise the Spirit helps us in our weakness; for we do not
> know how to pray as we ought, but that very Spirit intercedes
> with sighs too deep for words. (Rom. 8:26)

In my church's liturgies of confession, people's words of penitence are answered by God's word of forgiveness. The ancient world believed that divine words had power; they brought into being what they named. In Genesis, God spoke and the world was created. When God hears a confession of sin, his answer, "I forgive you your sins," creates a wholly new possibility. Because of Jesus' death and resurrection, there is no limit at all to God's forgiveness. No quantity or quality of sin is too much. God longs for us to come back, seeks us out, wants to reconcile us at any cost to himself. The forgiveness he gives is complete. At the end of time, at the Last Judgment, when the books are opened and everything known, we have his word that no charges at all will stand against us.

— Satisfaction: Struggling with Sin's Effects —

No one can make their sin up to God, or balance the books by piling up good behavior. The Reformation insisted that even to try to do so was itself sinful: obstinately doing ourselves what we must receive as a gift from Christ. Jesus' death and resurrection opened forgiveness as wide as the sky. There is nothing more to make up.

Yet making restitution to the people we have wronged is sometimes possible. God's forgiveness does not void justice. If I have damaged a colleague through slander, I owe her the truth. Obviously one cannot fully repay all such debts; ultimate justice is God's business. But peace with God brings its own yearning for wider reconciliation. We cannot rest easy with the booty of death if we participate in God's life.

Forgiven people find themselves in struggle. Nowadays we shy away from the warlike imagery of some of our old prayers and hymns, and no longer baptize people "manfully to fight under [Christ's] banner, against sin, the world, and the devil; and to continue Christ's faithful soldier and servant unto *his* life's end." Yet there is still a war going on. For someone raised in a racist world shaped by the deadly sin of anger, loving one's neighbor as one's self is a struggle every day. Working in an economy fuelled by avarice and envy, it takes energy to live out the message that life does not consist in abundance of possessions. Reconciled to God, agents of God's reconciliation, we still contend with our own resistance and the world's stubborn unwillingness to be reconciled.

Energy to persevere in that struggle comes from the Holy Spirit. Word, sacrament, Christian community, personal prayer and meditation all bring water to the well. Yet I am sometimes deeply discouraged by my own recalcitrance; I could record my confessions and play them to my confessor time after time, for all the change I see. But endlessly, boundlessly God forgives me. If the struggle with resistant evil makes me depend on God, the crucial battle is won.

Perhaps repentance may be understood better as pilgrimage. We have come a long way on our exodus. We have crossed the Red Sea, and we are free, forgiven, alive. But old habits die hard. On cold mornings our bones miss the heat of Pharaoh's brickyards; the taste of the leeks and garlic is still in our mouths. Sin is still savory.

Yet we are on the road. It has to be walked. We have to learn what it means to be free. We have to learn to live in covenant with God and each other, learn to hope and to do justice. We have to learn how to do without idols, without any identity or horizon but God. A promised land awaits. The journey requires perseverance: long, patient faith. When we lose the way, it has to be found again. When we are disoriented, we have to get direction. When we are tired, we have to ask for breath. The road has to be walked, from the city where the deadly sins reign to the city where God is the life of all who know him.

And the road itself is a gift. Jesus said that he is the Way, the road leading to God. God does not simply hand us a map with a list of turns on anonymous streets. Christ walks his way of the cross and resurrection with us, in us. Jesus also said that he is Life. God is not another taskmaster, flogging slaves into greater effort. He breathes his own breath of life—the Holy Spirit—within us. We walk along this road toward God, by God, through God.

C owley Publications is a ministry of the Society of St. John the Evangelist, a religious community for men in the Episcopal Church. Emerging from the Society's tradition of prayer, theological reflection, and diversity of mission, the press is centered in the rich heritage of the Anglican Communion.

Cowley Publications seeks to provide books, audio cassettes, and other resources for the ongoing theological exploration and spiritual development of the Episcopal Church and others in the body of Christ. To this end, it is dedicated to developing a new generation of theological writers, encouraging them to produce timely, creative, and stimulating publications of excellence, and making these publications available widely, reaching both clergy and lay persons.

241.3
STA

DATE DUE

241.3   13190P
STA   Stafford, William S.
        Disordered lives.
        Healing the seven deadly
        sins